SEASONS OF
LEARNING

SEASONS OF
LEARNING

TALKS TO GRADUATES
ON LIFE AFTER COLLEGE

V. A. Howard

PRAEGER

Westport, Connecticut
London

Library of Congress Cataloging-in-Publication Data

Howard, V. A. (Vernon Alfred), date.
   Seasons of learning : talks to graduates on life after college /
V. A. Howard.
     p. cm.
   Includes bibliographical references and index.
   ISBN 0–275–96102–8 (alk. paper)
   1. Life skills—United States. 2. College graduates—United
States—Life skills guides. 3. School-to-work transition—United
States. I. Title.
HQ2039.U6H68 1998
646.7′0084′2—DC21   97–22816

British Library Cataloguing in Publication Data is available.

Library of Congress Catalog Card Number: 97–22816
ISBN: 0–275–96102–8

First published in 1998

Praeger Publishers, 88 Post Road West, Westport, CT 06881
An imprint of Greenwood Publishing Group, Inc.

Printed in the United States of America

The paper used in this book complies with the
Permanent Paper Standard issued by the National
Information Standards Organization (Z39.48–1984).

10 9 8 7 6 5 4 3 2 1

To the memory of William James

CONTENTS

ACKNOWLEDGMENTS xi

INTRODUCTION 1

1 On Having a Mission 9

2 The Little Daily Tax 27

3 Catching On 47

4 Getting It Together 67

5 Toughing Out the Real World 89

6 Starting Over 109

SELECTED BIBLIOGRAPHY 135

INDEX 137

ACKNOWLEDGMENTS

In undertaking to write this book, I am presuming a great deal: first, that what I have to say will be of some value to those entering the workforce for the first time; and second, that the issues broached herein are perennial ones that—in slightly altered form–challenge succeeding generations of college and professional school graduates. Fortunately, I have had the opportunity—I might even say the honor—over thirty years of university teaching in three countries to confer with students, colleagues, parents, and employers on those issues of varying concern to them all. I like to believe that I have profited from that experience, and that it is worthwhile that I attempt to pass on in distilled form what I have learned. Certainly, I do not expect agreement on every or even major points; but if this book succeeds in prompting graduates and those who advise them to think more clearly about the future and their responsibilities to others and to themselves, it will have served its purpose.

In particular, I wish to thank my colleague and codirector of the Philosophy of Education Research Center at Harvard, Israel Scheffler, for his steadfast support and critical insights throughout the writing of this book. Jane Garry and Gillian von N. Beebe, my editors at Greenwood Publishing Group, saved the book from several gaffes and made many useful suggestions. Finally, to my many students over the years, but especially those in the Harvard University Extension who feel the pressures of work and study in their bones—thank you.

V. A. Howard,
Deer Island, New Brunswick

INTRODUCTION

GRADUATED LEARNERS

Seasons of Learning is about one of the more dramatic, difficult transitions most of us undergo in life: the transition from school to work. At the heart of that transition—more a transformation, really—are changes in the ways and reasons why we learn. The end of school hardly marks the cessation of learning but, rather, a new beginning, one fraught with much suspense and uncertainty. There is no escaping it.

That is the reason for this book: to examine that crossing. What happens when you cross the divide from learning for yourself to learning for work? "More than you could ever imagine" is the quick, intimidating answer. "Nothing you can't handle" is the more reflective response. Your education has prepared you for it in ways that have strengthened your resolve and capacity to cope, ways that will surprise you. In a word, you *can*.

While broadly concerned with learning's changing values in the loom of a lifetime, this book is addressed mainly to recent or soon-to-be graduates of colleges and universities. The book is also addressed to their teachers and advisors to whom it devolves to explain the realities of the workplace, so far as they

can. Guidance counselors, career consultants, corporate trainers, and personnel officers might also find the book useful to
analyze the fundamental issues confronting school leavers:
Must I have a mission in life? How do I find it? Will my values
change? How will I be valued once at work? Will anyone help me
to learn what I need to know, or am I going to be on my own in
a dog-eat-dog competition? What if I don't like the job? What if
I fail—how do I survive that? Should I put work before all other
considerations? What does it mean to succeed? How will my
commitments now affect my life later on? What's the use of all
my learning up to now? Must I give up my real interests to make
a buck? What becomes of *me* in all this?

Difficult, confusing, somewhat muddled, even impossible
questions they are, to be sure but, nonetheless, urgently felt by
those facing one of life's turning points. And they don't go away
just because a particular course of action has been decided upon.
Indeed, they may become even more acute once a choice of what
to do next has been made. After all, choosing a career path and
getting that first "real" job rank right up there with getting
married on any stress scale. Accordingly, a secondary aim of this
book is to raise the level of discussion with school leavers to
include those fundamental issues in a rationally reflective manner. To broach them, I shall argue, is to go to the heart of the
relations of education to life as well as to work. Conversely, to
ignore them in favor of the short view risks later regret, after
time and chance have taken their toll, and it may be too late or
too difficult to start over.

The specific audience of graduates I am addressing herein are
college- and university-level, adult school leavers entering the
workforce. That excludes both high school graduates, who have
their own special problems, as well as college or university
graduates moving on to further graduate studies or specialized
training. Not that all the aforementioned don't have similar
concerns, but those concerns are very differently manifested for
each cohort. That still leaves a sizable and diverse group. It
includes baccalaureates, master's students, and candidates for
or recent holders of the Ph.D. in all fields and disciplines. I also
have in mind graduates of vocational and trade schools, long-
term professional institutes, and executive training programs.

What they all commonly face is the adjustment from school to work or, perhaps, from some combination of school and work (so-called co-op education) to full-time work. Whether that adjustment uses things learned in school directly[1] or only indirectly or not at all,[2] the *context* of learning changes. It changes from the relatively "safe" environment of learning for its own or some postponed sake to the riskier, utilitarian, less protected work setting. Again, there is no escaping it, whatever the profession chosen.

As mentioned, learning hardly ceases in the shift from one setting to the other, as the misleading locution "So-and-so has *been* educated" might suggest. Indeed, learning may accelerate, but it does change, often drastically. At the very least, one is no longer in competition with others for grades and degrees but for positions, influence, and salaries. The range of personal choices to pursue one's own agenda may narrow even as the range of professional opportunities broadens. That may entail a complete refocusing of one's primary interests and learning entirely new skills, for example, actuarial or underwriting skills for the classics major entering a career in the insurance industry.

Even the Ph.D. in English Literature or the elementary school teacher trainee moving from one side of the desk to the other faces a critical period of adjustment to new responsibilities and tasks, often in places and institutions far removed from where he or she studied, away from mentors and friends, in challenging new circumstances—all of which greatly affect the pace and content of learning, not to mention the values attached to it. And not everything learned in such circumstances will be pleasant or helpful. As a side effect of getting the job, it's all too easy to overlook how the job may get us. At some point, for most of us, it becomes a forced option how and in what ways to reshape ourselves for employment. The following six chapters examine that passage from school to work and the changes in learning that occur, including the values that drive learning on both sides of the school/work divide and occasionally over it.

ORIGINS OF THE BOOK

Many of the topics and issues explored herein first emerged during consultancies to various academic and corporate organizations. They came into sharper focus during a 1990 summer Institute on Work and Education conducted by the Philosophy of Education Research Center at Harvard. Sponsored by the National Center for Research on Vocational Education at Berkeley, the Institute enrolled ninety teachers and administrators in corporate and vocational education from several countries. Participants examined in detail such topics as education and training, work in the new technological age, values and character in learning at and for work, and educating beyond technical skill.

From that time, I have had in mind to write a concise book of practical philosophy for graduates crossing the school/work divide. Based on several earlier studies of mine of learning in the arts and work,[3] my model is William James's 1899 *Talks to Teachers on Psychology and to Students on Some of Life's Ideals*.[4] In that delightful book, James undertook to explain the relevance of the fledgling science of psychology to teaching and to the knowledge base of teachers. In the concluding chapters, he explains to students, with great insight and modesty, the "practical applications to mental hygiene" of "certain psychological doctrines."[5] If only contemporary psychologists displayed such eloquent caution in the application of their theories to practical affairs; but we live in a thoroughly psychologized age in which the gospels of Freud, Piaget, Kohlberg, Bruner, Gardner, and a host of others compete for our attention in education. But James was also a philosopher, a pragmatist, and a thinker of profound insight into the practical affairs that shape our lives. His lead is the one I have chosen to follow.

I shall make no attempt to explain philosophy to students (they either know what it is or couldn't care less), but I will do a bit of it in an effort to clarify the "mental hygiene" of learning during the shift from school to work and thereafter. Accordingly, like James in his *Talks*, I shall strive to be practical above all without sacrifice of scholarly integrity while telling a lot of stories, drawing upon my own and others' experiences, to make a point. I shall address the reader directly, and the tone of the

book will be more assertive, less qualified, than a purely scholarly book would be. As does James's *Talks*, my book also selectively plunders earlier published material while reshaping it to
another purpose and audience. My goal is to help adult learners
to see through their odyssey to employment with a degree of
clarity about the choices involved in professional life and the
signposts of personal success or failure—in other words, to help
them get a focus on what is happening and where they are going,
like a navigator taking his or her bearings at sea.

In that practical spirit, this is an analytical, reflective work,
not a "how-to" manual of rules for success or survival. My
earnest hope is that it might be used by teachers and students
as the basis—as a point of departure—for serious discussions of
learning for life and work. Such discussions, in my opinion, are
best begun in school, in a supportive, critical atmosphere with
ample opportunity for open-minded give-and-take, before students are thrust out into the world. The hurly-burly of life will
ensure that they continue informally.

Some of what I have to say about aims, goals, strategies, and
the like, requires patience for simple abstractions for the sake
of eliminating the conceptual confusions that beset any transition in learning. I may even surprise the reader with frequent
talk about the arts; but there is a lot to be learned about
employment, about the application of oneself to a task, from the
experience of artists. Artists need expertise, and they need
devotion. They need judgment and experience. They must practice, and they must subject their efforts to scrutiny. There is far
more in common between the world of work and the work of
artists than is dreamt of in personnel policy.

Throughout, the emphasis will be on how values, in the sense
of goals, dispositions, performance standards, and their inter-
nalizations, shape and control learning. Closely related are the
changes that occur in personal knowledge and skills with growing competency and immersion in a task or job—a transformation of the self, not the mere tacking on of specific skills or
facilities to an unchanged and unchanging personality. All these
come together in one overriding theme: that the transition from
school to work entails a reconstruction of experience, as Dewey
would say, that marks the beginning of a crucial stage in a life's

course.[6] It's no accident that some college graduations are called *commencements* or what we might think of as a graduation (as on a scale) of learning, an adjustment of learning to new circumstances.

PLAN OF THE BOOK

It was my intention from the outset that chapter topics be cumulative in effect and concentric in structure, each subsequent one hooking back to earlier points and illustrations while elaborating new ones. The analogy I had in mind was that of a surveyor traversing the same variegated landscape from different starting points in order to create a grid map of the terrain. With each chapter the scale grows a little smaller, exhibiting more and more regional detail of interest. That way, I hope the reader will gain an overview of the logical geography of learning, its changing values as well as some of its enduring landmarks.

Accordingly, Chapter One, "On Having a Mission," takes the highest bird's-eye view of learning in terms of its aims, goals, and regulative values, including a few that tend to obscure the landscape below. Chapter Two, "The Little Daily Tax," moves in a bit closer on learning in terms of the commitments and costs that affect one's personal and professional life for good or ill, concluding with a section on what it means, what it demands of the Self, to be really good at something. Chapter Three, "Catching On," shifts perspective to the changing rhythms and modes of learning by instruction, by example (including imitation), and by apprenticeship. Special attention is given here to the different expectations and risks involved in school and work. Chapter Four, "Getting It Together," examines the changes that occur in the Self over time with the growth of technical proficiency and judgment. The hazards of burnout and the need for periodic modification of strategic and moral vision are also considered here. Chapter Five, "Toughing Out the Real World," surveys some of the economic, political, and social changes that are affecting businesses and the job market and the effects those changes are likely to have on worker behavior, loyalty, and ambition. In other words, what can someone starting out in today's economy reasonably expect? Finally, Chapter Six, "Start-ing Over," assays the uncertain present and near future in terms of the longer future certainty of having to let go of some of life's dreams and ambitions in a spirit of renewal and taking custody of oneself as well as of the next generation.

I would like to think that this is a book that the new graduate will keep on hand for piecemeal consultation in difficult times, less as a guide to action than as a stimulus to critical reflection upon the motives and consequences of the actions one has taken or proposes to take.

NOTES

1. For example, from a major in biology to a job as a field biologist or with an environmental survey firm.

2. For example, from a major in the classics to a job in an insurance firm.

3. See V. A. Howard, *Artistry: The Work of Artists* (Cambridge: Hackett, 1982) (hereafter cited as *WA*); V. A. Howard, ed. *Artistry: Varieties of Thinking* (New York: Routledge, Chapman & Hall, 1990) (hereafter cited as *VT*); V. A. Howard, *Learning by All Means: Lessons from the Arts* (New York and Berlin: Peter Lang, 1992) (hereafter cited as *LBAM*); and V. A. Howard and Israel Scheffler, *Work, Education, and Leadership* (New York and Berlin: Peter Lang, 1994) (hereafter cited as *WEL*).

4. William James, *Talks to Teachers on Psychology and to Students on Some of Life's Ideals* (1899; New York: Dover, 1992) (hereafter cited as *Talks*).

5. Ibid., p. 99f.

6. John Dewey, *Art as Experience* (New York: Putnam, 1958).

CHAPTER ONE
ON HAVING A MISSION

"I FELT I OWED IT TO MYSELF"

Everywhere in the corporate, political, and educational worlds, one hears talk of missions, of the necessity of having a *clear* mission that will provide direction, a sense of shared purpose, and results to be achieved. It's one of the first declarations one encounters in the workplace: "Our organization's mission is. . . ." Why not simply "aim," "goal," or "objective"? Certainly the four terms overlap willy-nilly in ordinary speech, but there is something particularly appealing in the word *mission* to large organizations and to those, large or small, of an ideological bent. One encounters less talk of missions among smaller, simpler organizations of decidedly practical purpose. The chief engineer of a land survey company would not likely open an interview with a job applicant by saying, "Let me explain our company's mission." He is more likely simply to say, "Here's what we do at Jones's Surveys," referring to the range of company activities.

I suspect that the appeal of mission talk to large, complex, often amorphous organizations lies in its religious and military connotations: a suggestion of lofty purpose combined with cogwheel, chain-of-command efficiency. Seldom is a company's mission statement negotiable despite that meaning of the term referring to a body of persons sent forth to negotiate as in "diplomatic mission." Rather, one is expected to approve the mission, to make a commitment (of faith?) to it as a condition of employment. That's at the highest levels of corporate rhetoric. Once the mission is declared and accepted, the conversation tends to take a rather more practical bent: Where do you see yourself fitting in? What are your qualifications [if it is an interview]? How is Division X doing? How can we increase efficiency [if it is a strategy meeting]?

Educational institutions have recently adopted the corporate mission rhetoric in their own ways. Where they used to speak of educational aims in the spirit of Plato, Aristotle, or White-head, they now tout departmental, school, or institutional "mission statements." The change is not insignificant, since, as mentioned, corporate mission statements tend not to be nego-tiable, at least not so readily, as aims conceived in a critical mode of inquiry and revision—as befits research and teaching. More-over, the chain-of-command and paramilitary connotations of mission talk seem especially inappropriate to academic institu-tions, unless, of course, one holds to the view that education is just another business or a wing of politics or of religion (all of which I would vehemently contest, but that is another matter).

Two other meanings of *mission* are directly relevant to the career choices and learning opportunities of recent graduates. *The Concise Oxford Dictionary* lists them as follows:

1. a task to be performed; journey for such purpose; military operation, esp. dispatch of aircraft or spacecraft;
2. a person's vocation or divinely appointed work in life.

Now, these are quite different undertakings. Elsewhere, I have argued at length that one's vocation (from the Latin *vocatio* or "calling"), what we sometimes call a "life's work," may differ entirely from one's job or tasks to be performed for remunera-tion and survival.[1] Both are called work, but they may be as dif-ferent as the labor required to ensure basic survival and the "labor of love" or devotion to task that issues in a painting, musical performance, or scientific theory. Occasionally, they coincide, as often happens in scientific, scholarly, or artistic careers; but just as often, they don't. Ask any taxi-driving, "out-of-work" actor. Better yet, ask anyone locked into a profession—it could be anything: law, medicine, teaching—that he or she has come to dislike. What started out as a labor of love may end by being just labor. There are those resourceful individuals, however, who can plunder their jobs for the sake of their vocations—the taxi driver–actor who studies his customer's accents and behavior for future roles, for example. Much subtler variations on this theme are commonplace.

Let me tell you about such a person, a true story. Theo, let us call him, graduated in philosophy with a Ph.D. from a prestigious eastern American university in 1970. I knew him well. To me, he seemed the epitome of the scholar. Gifted with a fine theoretical mind, he was also fluent in French, Greek, and German, widely traveled, and thoroughly knowledgeable in European literature and music. Theo's intellectual confidence and accessible personality were also strong assets for a career in teaching and research. He accepted a position with a large state university, where he quickly established himself as a highly respected teacher and scholar among his colleagues. The transition from school to work seemed effortless and virtually seamless. Even the introductory course in medieval thought he was required to teach came as an opportunity to expand his intellectual range. He appeared well on his way to joining the lucky few for whom job and vocation are coincident.

Then came the Organization of Petroleum Exporting Countries (OPEC) oil crisis of the mid-1970s, economic recession, followed by drastic cuts in university personnel. He was denied tenure on a technicality by a panicky administration. Within three months, Theo was out of a job and out of his vocation as well. Overnight, academic jobs dried up. What to do?

Ever confident of his intellectual abilities, Theo took the insurance industry's actuarial exams in Hartford, where he achieved a perfect score. "I've always been able to absorb technical materials easily," he later explained. He was quickly snapped up by a major insurance company and within a few years rose to the position of director of a research division. He read widely on business, probability theory, and demography and became expert on methods of trend prediction.

I ran into him again during the late 1980s when, through the auspices of a mutual friend, I became a consultant to his company on the so-called management process under Theo's direction. He seemed unchanged, ever curious, but strangely out of water in the glass and concrete corporate world. His obvious technical expertise and lightning computer skills were highly respected, but it was clear to me—and to him—that he would never rise above being a well-paid company "nerd," locked into middle management, despite his searing insights into the growing plight of the insurance industry. Company politics bored him, though he well understood such matters and the personal dynamics that drive them. He was simply not a player. None of that seemed to bother him and indeed enabled him to maintain a cool objectivity about the company's increasingly desperate "reengineering" and management process schemes. Quietly, his peers and superiors consulted him on technical as well as policy matters, knowing they would get an impartial view. Again, he appeared to have made an enviable adjustment.

I asked him about his intellectual life and was surprised to hear that he was still reading philosophy in depth, had become something of an authority on professional ethics, and had several articles in progress on corporate social policy. His grasp of literature led him to introduce novels and short stories into his training programs to great effect. Few of his innovations in corporate training, however, were either understood or appreciated by his employers despite notable improvements in morale and performance. To me, such obtuseness was disappointing, even stupid, given the company's financial deterioration and widespread inefficiency. (They eventually laid off 10,000 workers worldwide.)

Undeterred, Theo continued to devise new training programs, to attend technical conferences, even to conduct holiday excursions to European cultural centers for company employees on a volunteer basis—that is, until he was himself summarily laid off in late 1992. He is now seeking academic employment once again, hoping to make a lateral move into a business school at age fifty. With everything to offer, he has few prospects. He is an unorthodox candidate, a bad (and aging) risk from both business and academic points of view. The company's parting handshake was more bronze than golden: a year's partial salary, still better than what he got from academia.

However, even in unemployment, while he and his wife struggle along on a reduced income, Theo's passion for learning remains unabated. Amidst job hunting, he has managed to publish several technical papers, master the mathematical details of quantum mechanics ("because it is one of the great intellectual achievements of this century"), and commit to performance memory Beethoven's Second Piano Sonata! When I asked him how he has been able to persevere through all the changes and disappointments, his reply was as simple as it was telling: "I felt I owed it to myself."

Admittedly, Theo is unusually self-motivated, reminiscent, perhaps, of the poet Wallace Stevens or the composer Charles Ives, also insurance executives in their times (but comfortably employed). Like them, at least in this respect, the *value* that Theo attached to learning was adjustable to company interests but not limited to those interests. That was the secret of his success and sustained personal interest in business matters in good times and of his survival in bad times and, one hopes, in his future professional survival.

But note: The value of his learning to the company during his employment there was instrumental—his technical expertise, business insight, computer skills, and training abilities. Yet because he was able to generate an *intrinsic* interest in business matters, he was never reduced to thinking of his own learning as merely instrumental to company concerns. That way, he realized, lies drudgery and disappointment: treating your learning and expertise solely as means to others' ends; for when those ends are removed (or you are fired or retired), all motivation for thinking further about such matters ceases, often accompanied by a loss of self-esteem.

Theo's remarkable lack of resentment toward the company that fired him was due in part, I think, to his ability to relate the most mundane, practical aspects of his work for them to a broader context of learning. He construed such work as an investment in himself ("I felt I owed it to myself"), not *only* in the company. In the midst of his many company-related tasks, he found sufficient scope for his learning vocation in such ways as both to exploit it for company purposes and to sustain it beyond them. On the plane of self-development, Theo came away with far more than a bronze handshake, materially threatened perhaps but not psychologically undone like so many laid-off executives.

Does Theo have a mission in life? Hardly, in the sense in which that term now floats through organizational rhetoric. There is no chain of command directing his interests, nor is he pursuing them with quasi-religious or paramilitary zeal. His commitment to rational inquiry and disciplined self-expression (including his writing and musical practice) precludes both a purely instrumental approach to learning *and* an unquestioning allegiance to fixed institutional goals. Nor, of course, is he an addict of borrowed institutional prestige. His first loyalty is to himself in the best possible way.

It may be said that I am describing some idealized intellect. I am not. Rather, I am describing what a good liberal education is supposed to produce: a person of vision in the plain sense of someone with intelligent foresight and imagination, someone for whom learning is seen in the loom of a lifetime, not just a job, perhaps especially so when the going gets tough. I shall call this *learning with purpose*.

LEARNING WITH PURPOSE

Learning, of course, has many purposes; but I am proposing the phrase as just one way to bring some order to our talk of aims, goals, objectives, and the like, at the school/work divide. I am fully aware that ordinary speech tends to blur several of the distinctions I am about to draw, that terms like *aims*, *goals*, and *ends* float over them like seagulls over a school of herring, each word having its own vagrant etymology. No matter, it's the conceptual differences that matter, which differences, incidentally, are obscured by the military metaphor of missions tending to collapse everything into a chain-of-command hierarchy.

Learning with purpose, as an artificial construct, incorporates vision, aims, and goals, themselves somewhat simplified herein for practical purposes. Let us begin with goals.

Goals

A *goal* is a particular, tactical objective, specifiable in instrumental terms, for which there are equally specifiable means, sometimes called "success factors," that is, necessary and sufficient conditions for the goal's realization. Goals include problems and their solutions as well as skills and their acquisition. A typical problem requiring solution might be how to ensure no more than a 5 percent drop-off in service during an organizational changeover. A skill objective might be to bring participants in a computer training program up to a typing speed of sixty words per minute with fewer than five errors. The realization of goals also includes an assessment of "preventive conditions,"[2] whatever gets in the way of the realization of the goal. For example, will there be sufficient staff available during the organizational transition? Do participants in the training program already possess adequate reading skills to benefit from it? In effect, goals entail instrumental learning of a kind familiar to us all, often requiring instruction, practice, and drill.[3]

Aims

Aims as strategic ends or objectives are more general than tactical goals and sometimes have built into them certain principles of procedure, or normative conditions, regulating how they are to be achieved.[4] This is especially so in education. For example, if moral conduct among employees or students is our goal, then our aim of producing morally responsible individuals precludes such procedures as coercion, rote conditioning, or drugs. And that is because free choice and rationality are part of our conception of the moral life.

The logical result of such normative restrictions on the *manner* of doing things is that most disputes over the general aims of education (missions, goals, ends, if you wish) are in fact disputes over the means by which such broad outcomes as citizenship, moral character, cognitive perspective, and the like, are to be achieved.[5] Put another way, the more general the statement of the aims, the less likely we are to disagree over the aims as such and the more likely we are to disagree about how best to achieve them, precisely because the aims are built into the processes we employ to achieve them.[6]

In this way, general aims and values regulate the manner of doing things including the inculcation of those values. They are less goals (in the sense distinguished earlier) than "principles of procedure."[7] Conversely, where we do disagree over means *and* their separately identifiable (extrinsic) ends, the more likely we are to be talking about concrete, utilitarian objectives and facilities such as reading, writing, or computational skills and the best methods for inculcating them.

Outside education, in business or the military, or in other highly competitive enterprises, such restrictions on general aims such as profitability or victory may be less evident, perhaps lacking entirely. This is why, incidentally, as we approach a situation where the end justifies *any* means, we hear calls for ethical and legal restrictions on such activities. Witness, for instance, the sudden explosion of "business ethics" courses in M.B.A. programs in the wake of a series of Wall Street investment scandals in the 1980s, implicating some of the best young minds in the business.

These are two entirely different ways of looking at aims: those that are built into the means as basic values and those that are separable from the means as instrumental values (pure "how-to," no moral questions asked). Corporate and business aims tend to fall into the latter category: These are our aims. How do we get there? That is, business tends to assume that what it is doing is a "good thing" and just gets on with it. In a way, then, it makes more sense to speak of missions and goals, as external target states to be achieved, at the *higher* levels of corporate deliberations than at the higher levels of educational policy.[8]

By *higher levels* I simply mean at the level of their most general aims. For business purposes, learning is almost always instrumental. For education, it retains inherent value in the loom of a lifetime, a point of practical logic hardly lost on Theo ("I felt I owed it to myself"). Contrast Theo's motive with the motto of the famous Hudson Bay Company—Pro pelle cutem ("It wanted the skin for the sake of the fleece")—or the sometime slogan of the Du Pont Company—"Better Things through Chemistry."

Vision

As I shall use the term, *vision* refers to judgment and choice exercised at the highest levels of direction and review. It functions as a kind of critical overview within what Dewey calls a "means-ends continuum."[9] Therein aims, goals, and their respective means are continually revised in mutual perspective. That is, as competence and experience grow, as conditions change, so also does your entire conception of the tasks to be performed and the aims to be achieved. You might say that your interpretive abilities increase with practice, as when a musician strives for a better understanding of a particular piece of music.

I recall a recent television interview with (the late) distinguished conductor Sir Georg Solti in which he spoke of his lifelong struggle to improve his grasp of Beethoven's symphonies. For him, the works of the great composers represent limitless opportunities for growth in musical vision. Almost anyone who rises to prominence in a profession acquires such vision, although, as Theo's case poignantly illustrates, acquiring it is no guarantee of success or survival. There are just too many factors at work to speak of guarantees. Suffice it to say, without a developed and developing vision, top-level success is likely to elude you.

Vision requires imagination as a critical faculty.[10] It hovers over the entire enterprise from stem to stern, encompassing not only aims and goals but the broader context of institutional service and accountability to the members of the institution (or shareholders) and to the larger society. Vision is also a predictive faculty, a somewhat more than inductive capacity to "see round the corners." It may *feel* intuitive but is more likely to be the result of what the corporate world is fond of calling "environmental scanning"—the ability to take many, often unexpected, factors into account in pondering the future. Consider, for example, General Douglas MacArthur's comparison of China's war against the Japanese to the Russian defense against the Germans in 1941 (before that fatal winter campaign).

> China's defense has proved that a people with sufficient numbers, sufficient morale and sufficient space

> to retreat into simply cannot be conquered by any
> Blitz. On the base of China's defense I venture to
> predict that the German offensive against Russia will
> fail. Sooner or later, at this spot or that, it will bog
> down and peter out.[11]

This is a good example of what I should call *strategic* vision
of a sort highly prized in military, political, and corporate circles.
It is, of course, valuable in virtually any enterprise. But there is
another kind of vision, more appropriate to education, that I
should call *moral* vision, concerning what is inherently worthwhile for an individual or institution. It encompasses one's
highest calling (or vocation, previously mentioned) as well as
those aims, institutional or individual, that have their values
built into them. An example of moral vision, whether you agree
with it or not, is afforded by the late Albert Shanker, President
of the American Federation of Teachers, commenting on an
article by Dr. Sandra Stotsky[12] critical of the so-called multicul-
tural curriculum in elementary and secondary schools. Elaborating on Stotsky's criticism, Shanker says:

> Selecting works of literature that present the Ameri-
> can experience and American society in the worst
> possible light could have a number of bad conse-
> quences. Do we really want to encourage minority
> youngsters to focus only on the wrongs done to their
> group? Is it useful for them to see their identity
> primarily in terms of victimhood? And what of the
> non-minority students? A steady diet of books that
> inevitably portray their group as the villain could,
> Stotsky says, create self-loathing, as well as shame
> about their group and its heritage. It could also lead
> to the opposite—and this would be even worse. "How
> much shame and guilt," Stotsky wonders, "[can]
> white students . . . absorb before becoming hostile to
> the groups depicted in 'white guilt' literature?"
> Whatever the response of students, a curriculum of
> the kind Stotsky describes would exacerbate hatreds
> and tensions among groups.[13]

In some circles, Shanker, like MacArthur in 1941, might be ignored, even vilified, but that is just the point about moral vision: It continually, and in many different contexts, raises the question, What do we owe to ourselves and to others?

To that extent, moral vision is both self-centered *and* altruistic simultaneously, instrumental *and* concerned with ultimate values simultaneously. Now, I am in no position to say what those ultimate values are for any individual or organization, but rest assured that you, and the organization for which you work, have them, whatever they are. They may also be in conflict (imagine a radical ecologist working for a lumber company!). But for you, as a learner, the question of moral, as contrasted with strategic, vision is, What do I owe to myself? What you owe the company will, in any case, be largely determined by your instrumental worth to it in the realization of its strategic goals. The company's goals may or may not have anything to do with moral vision except as it conceives it, and that may or may not touch you at all as an employee. On the other hand, if you are an Albert Speer, a talented, young architect, seduced by his strategic vision and blind ambition into serving Hitler's heinous regime as Minister of Armaments, it would.[14] If, more likely, you are working for a company or organization whose strategic goals do not offend you, don't worry—keeping in mind, of course, that getting ahead and personal development (what you owe yourself) are not necessarily coincident.

A final point requires emphasis; namely, that the distinctions drawn here represent a logical plot of the overlapping ranges and relations of goals, aims, and vision, not a psychological sequence. Typically, the mind crisscrosses these domains in various directions, thus keeping thought dynamic, flexible, and sensitive to new information and possible revisions at every stage. Note them, but don't get fixated on them.

As a passing observation, I would add that several management process schemes I have examined tend to confuse the logical with the psychological. One hazard of that confusion is a tendency to become preoccupied with *where one is in the scheme* rather than the problem at hand. That's tantamount to corporate stage fright—an undue self-consciousness about *how* one should be thinking. Avoid it by treating all such schemes as aids to, but no substitute for, your own problem-solving abilities. Analytical categories are most useful when considered as a diagnostic gloss on thinking and learning at its best (or worst) rather than as a fixed series of steps to be followed. This caution flies in the face of the "quick-fix" mentality, but I offer it for what it is worth.

TRANSFORMATIONS

With these rough-and-ready distinctions in hand, we can begin to draw some general conclusions about learning with purpose and the transformations that occur across the school/work divide. First, the changes in direction and content may be negligible or at least highly compatible, as in Theo's first academic job or anyone finding employment in his or her field of academic specialty. Second, the direction may remain roughly the same while the content changes, as, for example, when an engineer shifts from one design area or company to another in, say, the aerospace industry. Third, the direction may differ while the content remains roughly the same, as in fiscal administration for profit or nonprofit organizations. And finally, both direction and content may change, as, for example, when Theo took a job with an insurance company. For most liberal arts graduates or nonspecialists moving directly into the workplace, changes in both the direction and content of learning are most likely.

Liberal arts graduates may appear to be at a disadvantage compared with specialists in the workplace, but that is to overlook their adaptability and exposure to a variety of fields and disciplines. One national Canadian magazine, for example, compiled an "Employers' Wish List" of desirable skills and qualities of "a top-notch employee" based on interviews with industry executives. The list included literacy, numeracy, ability to conceptualize and analyze, ability to think independently and creatively, and willingness to learn.[15] While the article lauded the advantages of co-op (work-study) programs, it failed to note that the qualities listed could be lifted from virtually any liberal arts college catalog.

Specialists may have an initial advantage, particularly in highly technical fields, but it is a documented fact that over two thirds (67 percent) of chief executive officers (CEOs) at least began with a liberal arts degree, whatever their subsequent professional training or degrees.[16] It seems that the surest route to the top begins from a broad base.

A few highly gifted or focused individuals may well know what they want to do with their lives by age eighteen or twenty, but even they can profit from broader exposure. Several years ago, I acted as consultant to the New England Conservatory (NEC) of Music in Boston on the nature and place of liberal studies in conservatory training. NEC's problem was opposite that of most liberal arts colleges. Instead of asking, What is the place of music (or other arts) in general education? they asked, What is the place of general education in specialized musical training? In effect, NEC was becoming concerned that its curriculum was too narrowly vocational in both senses of the term (job and "calling").

While most NEC students would rather spend more time practicing their instruments or studying composition, conducting, or music theory, the issue became acute for many near graduates as they contemplated employment prospects in the highly competitive (and small) domain of classical music. Most were not even equipped to teach music, despite their many years of intense training. Although I have seldom encountered an institution where the motivation to learn was higher, I was equally impressed by the growing desperation of many students on whom it was gradually dawning that they would not be the next Horowitz, Bernstein, or Sutherland. Driven as they were, many seemed to be driving themselves toward early "failure," again despite their high levels of musical competence. A tone of exasperation characterized their remarks: "This is what I *am* [a musician]!" "This is what I *do*!" "I don't *know* anything else!" I was reminded of those legions of black athletes in American universities or young hockey aspirants in Canadian schools, all hoping against hope to end up in the National Basketball Association (NBA), the National Football League (NFL), or the National Hockey League (NHL).

My recommendation to NEC's governing board was to include courses in history, philosophy, literature, and languages with electives in acoustical physics and mathematics (musical and mathematical aptitudes often go together)—all calibrated to music studies. My rationale was that the point of entry to such subjects was less important than exposure to them, even for those likely to make professional careers in music.

As might be expected, responses to my recommendations were more favorable among near graduates than among first- and second-year students. Surprisingly, however, the strongest support came from the elite few students destined for professional careers as symphony players, soloists, conductors, or composers. Their reasoning was practical and illuminating. "As a conductor with an international career ahead of me, I need to know at least two European languages other than English, preferably Italian and German," said one. "Musicians are temperamental, highly strung people. A knowledge of psychology and group dynamics would be a big help in getting along," said a cello major. A budding musicologist headed for even more specialized graduate studies complained of "knowing so little of the general historical background of the music I'm studying. What else was going on in Mozart's time in the other arts, literature, science, politics?" "I feel so *ignorant* of everything but singing," remarked a young soprano who had just won a major competition.[17] These were young people who knew full well what they owed themselves. Their strategic and moral visions had taken on an urgency that greatly enlivened their educational experience. A more seriously reflective group of disciplined professionals-in-the-making would be hard to find. I admired them and learned something from them or, rather, relearned something ancient.

What I learned from them is that Aristotle was right in thinking that theoretical, productive, and practical knowledge go together in the achievement of *arête*, or excellence. Aristotle distinguishes theoretical knowledge (*epistēmē*), aiming at truth for its own sake, what we would now call "science," from two kinds of "deliberative" knowledge: productive (*techné*), aiming at "making" something useful or beautiful, as in agriculture, engineering, or the fine arts—in effect, the exercise of trained skills of art and craftsmanship; and practical knowledge (*poli-tiké*), aiming at "doing" or action in relation to desire and moral conduct; that is, where we measure the consequences of our actions by their effects on the interests and welfare of others.[18]

The best students at NEC were intuitively aware that it was the blend of these three ways of looking at knowledge and training that would most enhance their own special *arête* as musicians. How best to accomplish that aim is perhaps less a matter of curriculum and courses than of attitude and disposition, which is to say, the propensity to see learning with purpose in that light.

Put another way, the old saw about experience being the best teacher is at best a one-third truth; for without adequate theoretical, productive, and practical knowledge (in Aristotle's senses), how are we to interpret that experience? What are we to make of it? How are we to assess its consequences for ourselves and others? No engineer, physician, or artist can even begin to practice those professions without adequate theoretical background, without extensive "hands-on" training, or without an eye to the consequences of one's vocational commitment. Certainly it is possible, indeed commonplace, to proceed blindly in pursuit of one's ambition (or that of others). And certainly it is advisable to follow your bliss wherever that is feasible in considering what work to do or calling to follow; but to do so unreflectively engenders hazards that might be avoided with a little of that combination of hindsight and foresight that we call imagination.[19] So much is perhaps obvious in the saying, but not so obvious in the doing, in the way that Artistotle had in mind. Seeing through to one's personal and professional *arête* requires considerable imagination across many factors, allowing also for time and chance to work their way upon us.

SUMMARY

I began this chapter with a criticism of the rhetoric of "missions" in education, particularly when contemplating one's own learning objectives at the school/work divide. In particular, I argued that mission talk obscures the role of governing values in education while reducing all means to a paramilitary chain-of-command hierarchy. The story of Theo's odyssey through the academic and corporate worlds served to illustrate the dividends, both personal and professional, of a commitment to learning for its own (and one's own) sake. Theo's story in turn led me to consider the idea of learning with purpose as a way of bringing some order to our thinking about the variety of purposes learning may have. I distinguished goals from aims from vision, the latter divisible into strategic and moral vision. Moral vision corresponds roughly to Aristotle's notion of practical knowledge wherein emphasis is on the long-term and moral consequences of virtually any undertaking. Describing the professional predicament of music conservatory students confronting their strengths and limitations, I tried to show the relevance of Aristotle's taxonomy of knowledge into three kinds—theoretical, productive, and practical—for resolving some of the difficulties of anyone, on any professional course, facing the transition from school to work. I finished with a reference to imagination as a critical faculty, and it is to that topic that I turn next under the aegis of what I call "the education of the sensibilities."

NOTES

1. Howard and Scheffler, *WEL*, chap. 1.
2. See Israel Scheffler, *Of Human Potential* (New York: Routledge & Kegan Paul, 1985), pp. 48–51.
3. See Howard, *LBAM*, chaps. 5 and 6.
4. R. S. Peters, "Must an Educator Have an Aim?" in his *Authority, Responsibility, and Education* (London: Allen & Unwin, 1959), chap. 7.
5. Ibid.
6. In John Dewey's words, "To set up any end outside education, as furnishing its goal and standard, is to deprive the educational process of much of its meaning, and tends to make us rely upon false and external stimuli in dealing with the child." From "My Pedagogical Creed" (1897), reprinted in Robert Ulich, ed., *Three Thousand Years of Educational Wisdom*, 2nd ed. (Cambridge: Harvard University Press, 1954).
7. Peters's phrase; see Peters, "Must an Educator Have an Aim?" p. 89.
8. It also needs to be said that *tentative* agreement on a mission in the sense of direction and coordination of effort is not incompatible

with critical revision later on, although that caveat seldom gets the attention it deserves.

9. John Dewey, *Theory of Valuation*, vol. 2, no. 4 of the *International Encyclopedia of Unified Science* (1939; reprint, Chicago: University of Chicago Press, 1966); chap. 6.

10. Howard, *LBAM*, pp. 13–14.

11. Quoted in Len Deighton, *Blood, Tears, and Folly* (New York: HarperCollins, 1993), p. 478.

12. Sandra Stotsky, "The Changing Literature Curriculum in K–12," *Academic Questions* 7, no.1 (Winter 1993–94): 53–62.

13. Albert Shanker, "Striking a Balance," *The New Republic*, 7 March 1994, p. 17.

14. See Albert Speer, *Inside the Third Reich* (New York: Macmillan, 1982), pp. 7–8, where he remarks on his early education and narrow ambitions.

15. *Maclean's Magazine*, 27 June 1994, pp. 32–33.

16. *Fortune* magazine survey; cited in Norman R. Smith, *How to Make the Right Decision About College* (New York: Wagner College Press, 1993), p. 77.

17. Personal interviews, 1986.

18. Aristotle, *Nicomachean Ethics*, Book 6. Ed. J. L. Ackrill (London: Faber, 1973).

19. See Howard, *LBAM*, pp. 13–19.

CHAPTER TWO

THE LITTLE DAILY TAX

DARWIN'S LOSS

In his *Talks to Teachers*, James quotes a famous passage from Darwin's autobiography in which the latter complains of the atrophy of his aesthetic sensibilities and tastes after years of scientific work. "My mind," wrote Darwin, "seems to have become a kind of machine for grinding general laws out of large collections of facts." Regretting the cost, Darwin continues, "If I had to live my life again, I would make a rule to read some poetry and listen to some music at least once every week; for perhaps the parts of my brain now atrophied would thus have been kept alive through use."[1]

Commenting on Darwin's loss, James remarks, "We mean all this in youth [to sustain our chosen interests] . . . and yet in how many middle-aged men and women is such an honest and sanguine expectation fulfilled? . . . We say abstractly: 'I mean to enjoy poetry. . . . I fully intend to keep up my love of music, to read the books that shall give new turns to the thought of my time.'" But that is just the catch: The intention remains an abstraction so long as "we do not begin *to-day*" (italics James's). "By neglecting the necessary concrete labour, by sparing ourselves the little daily tax, we are positively digging the graves of our higher possibilities."[2] Strong words in praise of small actions that can make all the difference.

Paying that little daily tax of extra effort is the price of educating our sensibilities in directions we should like them to develop. That, of course, applies to anything we should like to keep alive or to master, be it an exercise regimen, a special interest in music, birdwatching, or learning a language. Without payment of the little daily tax, one's expertise, and with it one's interest, dies. "Perhaps when I have more time, or when I retire," we say to ourselves; but that far-off "someday" sooner than later becomes no day when at last we realize that it is impossible, at least exceedingly difficult, to pick up where we left off years before.

I remember asking Theo how he managed just to find the time to keep up his varied interests in the midst of his demanding insurance job. He replied that instead of driving the hour commute to and from the office each day, he took the bus instead, thus assuring himself an interval of relative solitude for reading and reflection. Often, he used the time to catch up on work-related technical material but just as often to read Goethe in German or study a musical score. Thus did he avoid Darwin's loss and reap the benefits of the little daily tax.

One moral of this thrice-told tale is that habit is as powerful a force of exclusion as it is of inclusion. That is, we may disable ourselves by neglecting earlier acquired habits of mind or body even as we acquire new habits that enable us to perform different, usually work-centered tasks. In a word, we become lopsided. The point is not so simple *psychologically* as it is logically; for Mr. Postponement is forever whispering to us, "Someday," while the general wisdom of the Latin motto *Carpe diem* gets lost in the seizing of purely business or work opportunities. Such neglect may result in a subtle transformation of the Self amounting to professional development at the cost of personal atrophy of the kind that Darwin so poignantly regretted.

One more story to drive the point home before getting on to other, positive aspects of educating the sensibilities. My own near loss was exactly the opposite of Darwin's. For many years I harbored an interest in geology. Indeed, my first degree was in that subject. What with the demands of an earlier singing and later scholarly career in the arts and philosophy, my grasp of geology and *active* interest in it waned. Along with that extinction went a loss of pleasure in roadside and airborne observations that once enlivened otherwise tedious travel. In fact, it became irritating even to try to identify rock types and interpret structures no longer at my mental fingertips, as it were. So I gave it up altogether. I became a passive observer of pretty land and seascapes, a tourist.

Then, a few years ago, I found myself living for half the year in a geologist's paradise on an island in the Bay of Fundy. Increasingly frustrated by my habit-formed ignorance, I began reading once scrutable but now inscrutable technical reports on the area geology. Finally, I enrolled as a noncredit student in Harvard Extension geology courses in order, as I thought, to "brush up." I was astonished at the changes that had overtaken geology in my absence from the field. Much of my old "knowledge" was either flat wrong or obsolete, I discovered. Plate tectonics and satellite technology—the one barely a respectable hypothesis in my day, the other nonexistent—had transformed earth (and planetary!) science. After two courses and several guided field trips, I've rejuvenated or cast off a lot of old categories and theories and acquired many new ones as well as sharpened my field skills. I'll never be better than a rank amateur in an increasingly complex discipline, but much of the pleasure of casual field observations, attending lectures and conferences on special topics, and reading in the subject has returned. A wonderful series of guides to roadside geology, worldwide, are now available (thanks to computer technology), and I never leave home without one. As well, I've begun to notice unlikely links to my present work on learning, the discipline of the imagination (geology, after all, is a *science* of images), and the honing of performance and observational skills.

The morals of this little tale, as of the ones before it, are clear. First, you cannot just pick up where you left off. Things change. Second, once-accepted theories get revised or become obsolete in any developing field. Indeed, the expanse of one's *recognized* ignorance is an inducement to learn more. Third, "brushing up" in such circumstances is more like retooling oneself than mere recovery of old knowledge and skills. Fourth, there are unexpected, often surprising connections to be made with maturity between one's avocational interests and those of a more professional nature. And fifth, acquiring, sustaining, or recovering the "feel" of any field or discipline (including physical skills) is a matter of continued effort, of paying that little daily tax. The latter observation particularly brings me back to the main point of this chapter: the educating of the sensibilities whether at work or in the enjoyment of something for its own sake.

SCHILLER'S LEGACY

I borrowed the notion of educating the sensibilities from Friedrich Schiller's *Letters on the Aesthetic Education of Man.*[3] There Schiller refers to three kinds of education: for understanding, for morality, and for taste, wherein "the latter alone has as its aim the cultivation of the whole of our sensuous and intellectual powers in the fullest possible harmony."[4] Taste as interpretive judgment rests on sensibility construed as the *unity* of our capacities to think and to feel simultaneously. As I have written elsewhere, "sensibility is not a segregated faculty standing on its own awaiting 'synthesis' by yet another faculty of understanding [as in Kant's philosophy]. Rather, sensibility is a form of understanding, itself a 'synthesizer' of signs, signals, and clues variously cloaked, often inchoate and requiring reflective effort to interpret."[5] In practical and more familiar terms, sensibility issuing in judgments of taste comes down to whatever degree of "feel" one has for a particular subject or task, what Wittgenstein described as getting a "nose" for something.[6] That's what understanding, in the way that gets things done, is really all about.

Developing a nose for something might otherwise be described as a compound of productive knowledge and vision (both strategic and moral), discussed in the previous chapter. Accordingly, it is a mental commodity highly prized in virtually any serious undertaking. Recall, for example, General MacArthur's 1941 assessment of the German invasion of Russia. Commonly described by such metaphors as having "taste," a "nose" for something, or "gut feeling," it is sometimes called "intuition," or more plainly, "judgment." I prefer the Schillerian term *sensibility* to underscore the honed sensitivity required to apply general principles and knowledge to *cases* (as a good lawyer or judge might do) as well as to undercut the suggestion that taste is some high-flown, inborn instinct for the "better" or most expensive things. Rather, in my view, taste or judgment proceeds as much from the gut as from the mind—indeed, from both—and applies to practical as much as to theoretical or aesthetic matters and is less a product of mystery than of mastery.

To illustrate, I recently had occasion to confer with a local boatbuilder about the placement of a center console on a new oceangoing skiff that he was building for me. The question was, Should the console be placed amidships, as on most boats of similar design in the area, or slightly aft? Relying on tradition, I opted for amidships. My builder, defying tradition, preferred a placement about one third of the distance from the stern on the grounds that the weight distribution was better and would allow the boat to plane easier. In the end, I deferred to his judgment and discovered, much to my (and his) delight, that the boat did plane better than others of comparable design and was more stable. Beyond that, the aesthetic lines were much improved by what I (if not he) would describe as the principle of the Golden Section. Everything—from speed, stability, reduced fuel consumption, access to on-deck equipment, ease of control to appearance—was improved. Other boatbuilders and fishermen have come by to examine the innovation in detail. I take this to be a prime example of good judgment, of a refined sensibility and taste in such matters, not to mention a certain independence of mind.

John Dewey recounts a very different case in which a similar capacity to interpret subtle signals and clues based on past experience is involved.[7] He describes a routine job interview, which, although "disposed of as if it were an exercise in book keeping," is nevertheless "fraught with suspense" for interviewer and applicant alike. The former "sees by means of his own emotional reactions the character of the one applying. He projects him imaginatively into the work to be done and judges his fitness by the way in which the elements of the scene assemble and either clash or fit together." For the applicant, "the primary emotions . . . may be at the beginning hope or despair, and elation or disappointment at the close."[8]

However briskly dispatched, such a situation carries with it the possibility of "an interplay . . . in which a new experience develops" compounded, as we might now say, of cognition and affect. This is not to say that the interview is a wholly emotional encounter for either party but, rather, that the emotional *tone* of the encounter contributes to its significance and outcome for interviewer and applicant alike. "Where should we look for an account of such an experience?" Dewey asks. "Not to ledger-entries nor yet to a treatise on economics or sociology or personnel-psychology, but to drama or fiction. Its nature and import can be expressed only by art."[9]

By now, I can imagine your impatience. What does something as practical as a job interview have to do with art? It's one thing to speak of the "art" (with a small *a*) of a master boatbuilder, but to assimilate a purely business transaction to *that*? Supply and demand (plus credentials, of course) tell you more about the outcome of the interview than anything to do with art. Practically, I suppose that's true. Yet consider for a moment the appeal of the novels of, say, John Grisham, dramatizing some of the grimmer aspects of the legal profession (including the interview process); or those of C. P. Snow depicting academics, politicians, and scientists fighting it out for high stakes in committee! Whatever you may think of such works, what they attempt to do is to penetrate the seemingly humdrum surface of professional life to show us the drama beneath. Well, all that goes to show, you might reply, is that you can *make* a work of so-called fine art (good or bad) out of virtually anything, not that there is anything "artistic" about the original events themselves. A job interview or a government research committee in action is not art as such.

Granted. But it is not Dewey's claim that they are. Rather, his claim is twofold: first, that it is to the arts that we must turn to find an account of the *experiential* aspects of such events; and second, that notwithstanding the practical, intellectual, or political nature of such events, they all bear an "aesthetic stamp." Which is to say, to negotiate such events, to interpret the subtle clues, signals, or trends that animate and drive them, requires us, as we go along, to think with our feelings as much as with what we already know about such situations beforehand; in other words, to exercise our sensibilities in ways similar to how we might use them if we *were* confronting a work of art. In this sense, says Dewey, "the aesthetic is no intruder in experience from without, whether by way of idle luxury or transcendent reality. . . . [I]t is the clarified and intensified development of traits that belong to every normally complete experience."[10] "In short, aesthetic cannot be sharply marked off from intellectual experience since the latter must bear an aesthetic stamp to be itself complete."[11]

To bring this down to earth: If I understand him correctly, Dewey is saying that the aesthetic stamp may exist in different degrees of imprint, no doubt most conspicuously in art but elsewhere too—in practical and intellectual experience, not merely as a patina upon those experiences but as a seamless ingredient of them, what earlier I called getting the proper "feel" for a skill, discipline, or situation, or Wittgenstein's "nose" for something. In other words, not only the outcome and its causes concern us, as individuals wishing to influence that outcome, we want to know what it is like to go through such experiences with some degree of control over them.

LEARNING TO USE YOUR NOSE AND OTHER GOSPELS

Paying that little daily tax, and exercising your sensibilities with the growth of competency, is precisely what I mean by learning to use your nose. The important thing is to have *had* that experience, to recognize it for what it is, for what it is worth, if not to analyze it as I have done. The analysis is perhaps useful toward that recognition but is no substitute for it. The recognition comes from immersion in a task or discipline, when at last you realize that you have a grasp of the landscape, of the task to be performed, that you can move anywhere upon that landscape at will. It could happen anywhere: at school, at work, or at play—a feeling that you can move in one or another direction, come what may. That partly aesthetic sense of where you are in the midst of things is the core of what, by other labels, is referred to in the "Employer's Wish List" as the abilities to conceptualize and analyze, to think independently and creatively, and to be willing to learn.[12] The difference is that the latter list does not get *inside* the experiential base of what that means. Survival requires that you do just that. It's what your education up to now has been about: getting inside different forms of knowledge, expression, and learning.

This is not to substitute internal feelings of competency for objective standards of performance. Rather, it is to emphasize that until and unless one's sensibilities are engaged, such standards remain "out there," more rigid than flexible, more of a burden than an inspiration. Once inside a field or discipline, one works *with* as well as *up to* such standards.

Consider, for example, a classical singer learning a new song. First, there are the notes to be learned, then the text, not just the words but what they mean. At that point, one is on the brink of understanding the expressive content of the song. That in turn dictates the nuances of diction and phrasing. About here the singer's own sensibilities come into play as he or she seeks personal expression *through* the song and its text—more a matter of "finding one's own voice" for the piece, as singers say, rather than imitating the performances of others. Singers, musicians generally, speak of having made a piece their own, of "owning" it in the sense of having internalized its meaning and expressiveness so as to distinguish their several interpretations from each other's. Recall Sir Georg Solti's devotion to the symphonies of Beethoven mentioned earlier. Or consider these words of Oscar Peterson on knowing the landscape of jazz improvization: "A classical player is an interpreter. A jazz player is an instant composer—a Polaroid composer."[13] Knowing the landscape of any field or discipline like music comes with experience—but not just with experience: It comes through critical reflection upon that experience.

Compare now those examples with an internist's ability to interpret the plethora of symptoms that might indicate any number of diseases to arrive at a correct diagnosis. Physicians, too, make a certain speciality their own—gynecology, oncology— where their technical skills and knowledge are finely tuned to notice subtle signs that others less experienced, less immersed in that area, might miss. Even a general practitioner must become adept at first-line detection in order to refer the patient to the appropriate specialist—rather like a composer or conductor who must rely on the expertise of many musicians performing on different instruments. Boatbuilding, job interviewing, singing, jazz improvization, rendering a medical diagnosis—each, however different in most respects, places special demands on the sensibilities of those who would do it well.

Even were you to agree with my rather eccentric emphasis on the role of the sensibilities in learning at school or at work, you might still object that I appear to be advocating a relentless, nearly obsessive, time-on-task view of things; that so preoccupied am I with paying the little daily tax that I have lost sight of what James in another fine phrase calls "the gospel of relaxation."14 The latter is his antidote to "those absurd feelings of hurry and having no time."15 "It is your relaxed and easy worker," he continues, "who is in no hurry, and quite thoughtless most of the while of consequences, who is your efficient worker; and tension and anxiety, and present and future, all mixed up together in our mind at once, are the surest drags upon steady progress and hindrances to our success."16

I quite agree with James on this point, and it may surprise you that I am prepared to carry his gospel of relaxation one step further, to the extent of advocating idleness as a necessary (though hardly sufficient) condition of the cultivation of our sensibilities in any given domain. Now, how can this be? By all dictionary accounts, and by common consent, idleness is the moral and conceptual opposite of work or getting anything done. Among its synonyms: *inactive, useless or groundless, lazy, indolent, shiftless, to pass time without working, ineffective, vain, worthless, having no special purpose*.17 Idle time, idle talk, idle curiosity (noseyness, daydreaming), idle hands, all the devil's workshop. Idleness appears to have no redeeming virtues.

So threatening is idleness to productivity and morale that its mere *appearance* at school or in the workplace is to be avoided at all costs. This extends even to absurd details. One major corporation I recently visited has no memoranda, only "Action Slips." I was reminded of Heinrich Böll's satiric short story "Action Will Be Taken"18 in which the protagonist, basically a lazy fellow, masters the facade of looking busy at work while his frenetic boss runs about urging one and all, "Action will be taken! Action will be taken!" So successful is he in the art of dissembling that he rises to a high position in the company. When the boss suddenly dies of a heart attack induced by overanxiety, he is assigned to be a pallbearer. At the funeral, the employee's lugubrious performance as a pallbearer is so convincing that the mortician offers him a job as a professional mourner, a position he quickly accepts as being more congenial to his indolent nature!

Similarly, many of the people I observed in the multinational corporation I visited hustled from one tightly scheduled meeting to the next, exchanging "Action Slips" and complaining of "having too much on my plate" to consider anything but the most pressing business at hand. In the meantime, senior management complained of being deluged with unclear, hastily conceived documents that consumed a disproportionate amount of their time in the sifting. My observation that many people in the company appeared to work harder at being busy than at being productive was met with puzzled skepticism. How could that be when everybody was constantly encouraged to be "quick, flexible, and right?" Action never ceased being taken.

The fear of appearing idle, even in leisure, generates its own excess of activity, perhaps best captured by the "work hard/play hard" ethos of modern consumerism. The casualties of frenetic activity for its own sake are reflective thought, on the one hand, and significant experience, on the other. As Dewey once remarked, "Zeal for doing, lust for action, leaves many a person, especially in this hurried and impatient human environment in which we live, with experience of an almost incredible paucity."[19] Every obstacle exists only to be beaten down, seldom as "an invitation to reflection. An individual comes to seek, unconsciously even more than by deliberate choice, situations in which he can do the most things in the shortest time."[20]

In effect, nothing matures, no thought, act, or experience; for instead of reflection, further action must be taken. Yet the biographies of artists, philosophers, scientists, and military and political leaders are strewn with references to the idle thought, idea, or daydream that proved a turning point in their lives and work. From Saint Paul's vision on the road to Damascus to

Descartes's dream of the "geometric method" to Francis Crick's "gossip test"[21] for assessing the significance of scientific ideas, idleness—literally, the idling of the mind, like a machine out of gear—has proved decisive. The free rein of the imagination in relaxation is a creative by-product of "doing nothing."

During idle moments of daydreaming or reverie, even of pure escapist fantasy, we are never quite doing nothing. We continue to reflect upon and to respond to our experience, perhaps even reshaping it to suit our whims. The mind airily floats down corridors of discovery and possibility opened, no doubt, by wishful thinking, where not *every* dream is Walter Mitty-esque, but some may take root in reality.[22]

It is difficult for those committed to the gospel of work as action to see much value in James's gospel of relaxation except as restorative "time off" as opposed to time on task. But not all that is idle is *mere* rest and recuperation; idleness can also be a stimulus to the imaginative refinement of experience, ideas, and dreams that might otherwise go unexplored. Intelligent action will be taken when once we learn to encourage idleness and even the wildest flights of imagination as sometime "reality checks" to relentless time on task; for the purely imaginary in fancy may turn out to be the usefully imaginative in reality.[23] That, too, is part of the gospel of learning to use your nose as much as paying the little daily tax.

ON BEING WELL PRACTICED

One of the ways we learn to do things well, particularly routine things, is to practice them. Such practice may be preparatory, as in running scales on a musical instrument or repeating vocabulary in learning a language; or it may come in the natural course of performing certain tasks, like underwriting insurance claims or speaking the language, on a regular basis. Educators nowadays are fond of calling this "learning by doing" or "hands-on" experience. It is the centerpiece of so-called co-op education or work-study programs designed to give people real work experiences to complement their academic studies. At their best, such programs carry theory into practice and back again. At their worst, they become myopically narrow in focus, resulting in the acquisition of skills irrelevant, or soon to be obsolete, in the workplace. Such obsolescence, incidentally, has been a liability of vocational education throughout its history.[24]

Rather than launch into criticism or celebration of one or another such program (the Germans, Japanese, and Scandinavians seem to excel at them), I prefer to ask, What does it mean to be well practiced at something? What does it mean to practice well? Both questions are ambiguous as between being well *drilled* and being well *trained*; and this is an important distinction, for drill and training, although closely related, are not the same. The confusion comes about from the notion, correct so far as it goes, of practice as learning by repeated trial or performance. Left at that, however, significant differences in *what* is learned are obscured.

Drill aims at the acquisition of certain habits, routines, and facilities like learning the alphabet, multiplication tables, typing, or good posture, until, as we say, they become "second nature." Training, on the other hand, while it involves drill, also requires "stimulation by criticism and example of the pupil's own judgement."[25] In other words, training aims to impart critical skills that demand judgment and choice both in their acquisition and, more important, in their deployment.[26] Skill at boatbuilding, for example, involves plenty of facility in the use of a variety of tools and materials; but it also involves judgment in how to deploy them, as the earlier example of my boatbuilder's decision to place the console further aft than normal illustrates nicely.

Now, it is an all-too-easy step from that observation to infer that drill is an entirely passive affair even if training, overall, is not—that is, to conclude that "drill dispenses with intelligence," whereas training develops it.[27] Such a view, however, misrepresents both the process and the results of practice. Consider, for example, the first stages of learning a language. New sounds, vocabulary, and syntax have to be mastered through constant repetition and cross-references to one's own native tongue. Gradually, vocabulary and syntax come together to form sentences, awkwardly at first, but then with greater fluency as one goes along.

But note, routinization of vocabulary and syntax by drill is an *achievement*, usually the result of considerable exercise of attention on the part of the learner and careful intervention by an instructor. Achieving a proper accent, learning verb forms, vocabulary, and the like, requires one to hold specific ends in view through trial after trial until errors are recognized as such and eliminated. If routine response is the outcome, such response hardly "dispenses with intelligence" in the making.[28]

The achievement of being able to do something "in one's sleep" or "without thinking about it" is purchased at the price of wakeful vigilance en route. Otherwise, drill, construed as *mere* repetition, stamps in mistakes as readily as right responses. In the words of Francis Bacon, "If a man that is not perfect be ever in practise, he shall as well practise his errors as his abilities and induce one habit of both; and there is no means to help this but by seasonable intermissions."[29] Practice makes perfect only if it is not blinded by the lack of seasonable intermissions of critical intelligence. Which is to say that drill and training grade one into the other by the exercise of mind over the matter of repetition.

So, how do drill and training combine with the sensibilities in fluid performance? I can think of no better answer to that question than the one given by Bill Evans, the late jazz pianist, during an in-depth interview with Marion McPartland shortly before his death.[30] "Basic structure," said Evans, is crucial to putting together a jazz ensemble performance of even the simplest tune, for example, a C Major to C7 chord progression over a pedal point. Mastery of such a structure provides "a plane or bottom," Evans said, from which the rest of the piece springs. Thereafter, "intuition has to *lead* knowledge, but it cannot be out there on its own." This from one of the most "spontaneous" performers in the business! Evans's hard-won mastery of basic structures enabled him to commit to routine aspects of musical performance that others, still learning, may find exceedingly difficult.

"The great thing in all education," says James, "is to *make our nervous system our ally instead of our enemy*."[31] On the way toward mastery, to being well practiced, *"Never suffer an exception to occur till the new habit is securely rooted in your life.* Each lapse is like the letting fall of a ball of string which one is carefully winding up: a single slip undoes more than a great many turns will wind again. Continuity of training is the great means of making the nervous system act infallibly right."[32] Moreover, routine is relative: relative to one's level of expertise and achievement. One person's routine will be another's desideratum, and constant vigilance through the acquisition of routine is a condition of success. Why else, for example, would the conservatory students I interviewed demand such seemingly disproportionate amounts of time for practice?

So even as training is irreducible to routine response, neither is drill, notwithstanding the latter's *achievement* of routine response; neither is routine response entirely absent from the achievements of training in exercising the skills of performance. Intelligence *and* routine are to be found at both ends of the practice spectrum—in drill and in training—despite their different emphases and outcomes. If intuition (what I call sensibility) is to lead knowledge and skill of execution, as Evans suggests, it can only be on the basis of critical attention to detail—what we call learning from our mistakes—at every step of the way. As I have put it elsewhere, "Drill . . . is one of the most powerful, intelligent, imaginative means of learning at our disposal, enabling us to master the facilities required by advanced skills. Through drill we not only learn by example and instruction, but become examples of the very things we learn. One might even think of this as the existential predicament of learning anything at all: you are what you learn to do routinely."[33] That is what it means to be well practiced and to practice well.

ON BECOMING WHAT YOU DO

Paying the little (or not so little!) daily tax has two broad effects: One, of course, is the growth of proficiency at one's chosen task or discipline; the other is a rather more subtle transformation of the Self. We are accustomed to think of skill acquisition as mastery of a "bag of tricks" of the trade, whatever it is, and of skills themselves as "tacked on" to a mostly unchanged personality—rather like putting on a new suit. This is another of those half-truths at best, like practice construed as bovine persistence, that haunt our views of learning. Against that caricature recall the despairing remarks of the music conservatory students threatened to the very core of their being by perceived limits on their performance abilities and prospects. "This is what I *am*! This is what I *do*!"

Familiar enough as a psychological affliction of adolescents, adults are equally susceptible to the angst of limits real or imagined on their abilities. The executive who loses his or her job loses not only a livelihood but also a way of life that up to then has been a source of self-esteem, even of self-identity—so wholly do we become identified with the work we do. Similarly, the burned-out politician, professor, or social worker may suffer acute disillusionment—so wholly do we idealize as well as identify with our chosen work.

One is reminded of those closing-night blues of actors and singers in which the characters they have been portraying and the world in which they existed come to an abrupt end. I recall my own genuine sorrow several years ago at the breakup of the cast of *The Roar of the Greasepaint, the Smell of the Crowd*, after a sixteen-week run in which I played the role of the lovable/hateable "Sir" with a large chorus of altogether lovable and talented children. To many of them, I *was* "Sir" but only in my makeup. They took little notice of me in mufti until I came out of the dressing room heavily padded around the middle, in morning clothes, spats, shooting stick, and top hat with a purplish nose and mutton chops sprouting from the sides of my face. Gleeful pandemonium backstage! It was like playing Santa Claus night after night to (and with) an adoring entourage.[34] What person of normal sentiment would not identify with such a role? Consider, then, the threat to one's self-identity and self-worth of the cessation of sixteen or thirty years in a professional role. It can fall like the sword of Damocles, unless . . .

Unless, like Theo, one's learning with purpose includes more than just the job at hand. Learning with purpose, you will recall, entails vision both strategic and moral wherein the latter (moral vision) encompasses what you owe to yourself as well as to others in the way of self-development. For the moment, however, I am less interested in the cure than the causes of the constricted Self—the self all too reduced to a professional role.

A condition of self-atrophy can come about in any number of ways, and there are any number of ways of describing or accounting for it. Darwin, for example, spoke of neglect of his aesthetic sensibilities. The tack I shall take is to focus on the *social imagery* of certain professional practices.[35] Initiation into any complex field or discipline entails not only mastery of a variety of facilities and skills but also conformity to a host of sometimes conflicting standards and preconceptions of what those practices are or ought to be. Rightly *and* wrongly, narrowly *and* broadly, certain norms of conduct and procedure attach themselves to what it is to practice law or medicine, to be a musician or an IBM executive. The so-called corporate image, for example, encompasses everything from educational background and training to sartorial style and comportment. "Schools" of training and instruction in music, architecture, science, business, and the like, promote quite different conceptions of the "done thing," of what is customary in the way of *the* practices to be acquired and mastered.

Now, there is nothing inherently wrong or limiting in any of this; for, as Francis Crick reminds us, it is conducive to good work in theoretical physics that scientists keep company with other scientists, not merely to read the results of others' work but to get to know other scientists better in order to see how their minds work, including their strengths and limitations.[36] Science, after all, is a competition of ideas as much as business is a competition for profits; so it is important to be in touch with the nerve centers of major activity and to be perceived, oneself, as a participant in those activities. So far, so productive and enlightening.

On the other hand, the fact that some of the social imagery of certain fields or occupations may turn out on closer inspection to be utter nonsense, prejudicial, or obscuring (such as overuse of "buzzwords" and professional jargon) is very much to the point. For what starts out as initiation into the accepted, proven-effective practices and procedures of any given field may turn into a straitjacket of conformity. That applies as much to social revolutionaries, to scientists and intellectuals, as to the most conservative defenders of the status quo. Witness the recent wave of "politically correct" conformism on American campuses or the snooty suspicion of research scientists toward any of their number who may feel a responsibility to communicate outside the Select Circle.

Academics are no less prone to absurd extremes of conformism than other professionals. In the 1940s and 1950s the personal habits and mannerisms of philosopher Ludwig Wittgenstein enthralled a generation of Cambridge students to the extent of their imitating his Austrian speech patterns, ubiquitous leather jacket, and abrasive manner, often at the price of their own budding abilities.[37] In the corporate and business worlds the model of car one drives, the cut of one's suit and color of tie, how one talks and plays the game, choice of drink or cigar, may come to crowd out more essential concerns, depending on the degree of social pressure driving them. Style comes to substitute for substance.

Whether prudent, conducive to cooperation, inspiring, or positively inhibiting, such social imagery in the arts, sciences, and professions comprises a fabric of suggestion and preconception of varying regulative force. For good or ill (and probably both), social imagery helps to shape and direct the practices within a given field: how they are seen, how they are done, and how they are taught. They also shape the Self that identifies with them in terms of hopes, expectations and aspirations, and everyday behavior. Thus may the Self be transformed by what one does for a living, again for good or ill. The fact is that such transformations are an inevitable by-product of learning at any stage of life: in Melville's poignant words, "[T]hrough infancy's unconscious spell, boyhood's thoughtless faith, adolescence's doubt (the common doom), then skepticism, then disbelief, resting at last in manhood's pondering repose of If."[38]

Whether that "If" sustains an autonomous Self able to rise above conformity and narrowness or becomes filled with Kipling's urgency "to fill the unforgiving minute" with trivia brings us back to the fundamental relations between work and education in what I have been calling learning with purpose. To summarize those relations:

First, work is not a simple or univocal concept. Trade, occupation, or job does not exhaust the concept, which also includes "vocation" (or calling) in the sense of a life's work. Accordingly, second, educating for work is not reducible to training for a livelihood, important as that may be, but inevitably includes educating for a way of life, maybe even a life's work. Third, anything, even the most distinguished of "careers," may become drudgery under conditions of tiresome routine, conformity, or no growth. Fourth, finding a work to do, grandiose as it may sound, is virtually synonymous with finding a way to live. One's job may or may not support that way to live, but the choice of how best to spend one's life is of the highest personal and educational responsibility—one that learners and educators alike cannot escape. Finally, *educating* for work, as contrasted with training, is a moral responsibility that entails the inculcation of perspective (that is, vision both strategic and moral) so that individuals can see not only *how* to do well but what to do and why.[39] If, to a large extent, you are what you work at in life, it pays to reflect on the consequences of where you shall pay that little daily tax.

SUMMARY

I began by commenting on Darwin's loss of his aesthetic sensibilities through failure to keep them alive by what James called paying "the little daily tax." I went on to observe that postponement of that tax usually amounts to a permanent debit in one's personal development, recoverable only by a far greater effort than it would have taken to sustain them. In the spirit of Schiller and Dewey, I evoked the notion of the education of taste, of superior judgment or sensibility as the unity of our capacities to think and feel simultaneously in any given domain—to get the "feel" or a sense of the landscape of one's activities, most particularly, that of a chosen field, discipline, or occupation. This in turn led to my advocating greater attention (by oneself, as a personal matter) to the "aesthetic stamp" on otherwise practical affairs as a component of learning with purpose. Recognizing the asethetic stamp in what we choose to do helps us to understand what it means to acquire a "nose" for something, to be able to perform with confidence and versatility under varying conditions at most tasks, practical or theoretical, professional or avocational. I then took issue with the bad reputation of idleness in our society, indeed, recommending it as an imaginative "reality check" on relentlessly narrow time on task. To balance the picture, I asked, What does it mean to be well practiced and to practice well? Noting the differences between training and drill and their respective results, especially the former's issuing in *critical* skills, I concurred with James that their overall purpose is to "make habit our ally instead of our enemy" in the growth of competency at virtually anything that seriously engages us. Finally, I considered the pros and cons of self-absorption in the procedures and practices (the social imagery) of various occupations—how they may work for or against us, both as regards how well we do at that job and the effects on our selfhood, on character and personality. I dwelled largely on the liabilities of such conformity, while noting its advantages, out of wary respect for the power of habit, especially over long periods, to shape the Self in ways irredeemable.

NOTES

1. Quoted in James, *Talks*, p. 36.
2. Ibid., p. 37.
3. Friedrich Schiller, *Letters on the Aesthetic Education of Man*, trans. Reginald Snell (1796; reprint, New York: Frederick Ungar, 1965).
4. Ibid., Letter no. 27.
5. Howard, *LBAM*, p. 40.
6. Ludwig Wittgenstein, *Philosophical Investigations*, trans. G.E.M. Anscombe (1953; Oxford: Blackwell, 1976), p. 228.
7. John Dewey, *Art as Experience* (1934; New York: Putnam, 1958); pp. 42–43.
8. Ibid.
9. Ibid.
10. Ibid., p. 46.
11. Ibid., p. 38.
12. See Chapter 1, p. 20.
13. Oscar Peterson in an interview on the CBC (Canadian Broadcasting Corporation), 5 August 1994.
14. James, *Talks*, pp. 99–112.
15. Ibid., p. 108.
16. Ibid.
17. *The Concise Oxford Dictionary*, 9th ed.; and *The American Heritage Dictionary*, 3d ed.

18. Heinrich Böll, "Action Will Be Taken," in *The Art of the Tale*, ed. David Halperd (New York: Penguin, 1987).

19. Dewey, *Art as Experience*, p. 45.

20. Ibid.

21. Francis Crick, *What Mad Pursuit: A Personal View of Scientific Discovery* (New York: Basic Books, 1988), p. 17f.

22. Cf. Israel Scheffler, *In Praise of the Cognitive Emotions* (New York: Routledge, Chapman & Hall, 1991). "Sometimes the best approach is to turn away from it [the problem] completely, let the mental machinery idle, go for a walk, take in a movie, have a cup of cocoa" (p. 137); also see Bertrand Russell, *In Praise of Idleness* (1935; London: Unwin Hyman, 1976).

23. Cf. Dewey on the imaginary and the imaginative in *Art as Experience*, pp. 267–69.

24. W. Norton Grubb and Marvin Larzerson, "Rally 'Round the Workplace: Continuities and Fallacies in Career Education," *Harvard Educational Review* 45, no. 4 (1975): 451–74.

25. Gilbert Ryle, *The Concept of Mind* (1949; Chicago: University of Chicago Press, 1984), pp. 92–93; see also Israel Scheffler, *Conditions of Knowledge* (1965; Chicago: University of Chicago Press, 1986), p. 103.

26. Howard, *LBAM*, p. 99.

27. Ryle, *The Concept of Mind*, p. 43.

28. Howard, *LBAM.*, pp. 99–100.

29. Francis Bacon, "Of Nature in Man," in *The Essays of Francis Bacon 1561–1626*, ed. John Pitcher (New York: Penguin, 1985).

30. Aired on CBC, 30 July 1994.

31. James, *Talks*, p. 34; italics his.

32. Ibid., p. 35; italics his.

33. Howard, *LBAM*, p. 103.

34. The nineteen-year-old lad, incidentally, who played "Cocky" to my "Sir" in the musical game of life was Victor Garber, now a Tony Award winner and veteran of many Broadway shows.

35. Howard, *LBAM*, pp. 92–95.

36. Crick, *What Mad Pursuit*, p. 17.

37. See Gary Wills, *Certain Trumpets: The Call of Leaders* (New York: Simon & Schuster, 1994), pp. 171–72.

38. Herman Melville, *Moby Dick* (1851; reprint, New York: Signet, 1980), chap. 114, "The Glider," p. 464.

39. See Howard and Scheffler, *WEL*, chap. 1, "The Language of Work," pp. 7–26.

CHAPTER THREE

CATCHING ON

TWICE UPON A LIFE'S TIME

For most people, there are two great breaks in the momentum of learning in a lifetime: once when they leave school for the last time, be it from high school, college, graduate school, or professional school; and again when they retire or lose their jobs. Both experiences, for many people, are like a boat losing power at sea or a runner breaking stride in midrace. In extreme cases, they may resemble more a post partum depression, a tremendous feeling of letdown and loss even as new stresses are developing. There may be, in fact, several such breaks in the rhythm of learning, depending on how many changes in educational direction or jobs one makes. Then there are the many demicadences that accompany the shift from one subject matter to another or from one occupational task to another. In each case, the regaining of momentum is a matter of catching on to the demands, challenges, and responsibilities of the new domain. Since these chapters are mainly addressed to students, I shall keep the focus on the transition from school to work.

I deliberately chose the phrase *catching on* for its common currency to describe the beginning of understanding but also for the suggestion that what is caught on to has a forward momentum of its own. Catching on to a new field or job is at times a bit like chasing a departing train down the platform and jumping on before it gets away. How do we catch on? Usually, by a combination of formal studies or instruction (if the field is a complex one like medicine or law), practice in ways already described, example, and apprenticeship, to mention a significant few.

While differing among themselves, these ways of catching on overlap in experience, creating some confusion about the expectations appropriate to each of them. For example, in matters of practical ability, one often hears it said, "She didn't learn that in school or from books." Or, "Only experience can teach you that." On the other hand, there are many things that can *only* be learned in school or from books: the elements of quantum mechanics or legal torts, for instance. And what, after all, does it mean to say that some things come only with experience? Do they come automatically? Apparently not, given the range of abilities that emerge from experience among individuals. What can be done by oneself or with the aid of others to enhance that experience—to get the most out of it? These are some of the questions I want to address here in terms of the relations among the different ways of catching on mentioned earlier.

CATCHING ON BY INSTRUCTION

In Israel, the Mandel Institute for Advanced Studies in Education recruits people from such diverse fields as medicine, anthropology, science, law, and of course, teaching for future high-level careers in education—especially in administration, policy, and planning, what is generally called "educational leadership." The program consists roughly of three parts: academic studies in educational history and philosophy, psychology, and specialized research methods appropriate to the candidate's interests; case studies and individual research projects (also calibrated to the candidate's special interests); and field experience lasting up to a year in a kind of apprenticeship capacity.[1]

What I find intriguing from a learner's standpoint about the Mandel program is its emphasis on the development of an educational vision (in the senses of Chapter One) combined with practical expertise and guided field experiences. All the proven ways of catching on are utilized extensively: from formal instruction to applied research, to practice in case analysis, to learning from the example and advice of others experienced in one's chosen area of concentration. In the final phases, participants are literally "coached" into expertise, like an opera singer preparing for a role. Each of the ways places different, if complementary, demands and expectations on the learner. You can expect to go through something like the Mandel program even if rather more haphazardly in the course of your own professional growth. So let's see what the different elements contribute.

First off, what can one expect of instruction whether in school or on the job? The first thing to say is, not everything but a lot. So what *is* instruction? The answer to that question is that instruction comes in many forms: from recipes for chocolate cake or assembly instructions for a stereo system (for which no instructor is required) to purely how-to training (usually by an instructor) in such facilities as swimming or computer skills to sustained *dialogue* between teacher and students on such controversial topics as the role of education in developing societies or the directions of applied research.

The latter, dialogue, points up an important difference between teaching, generally, and instruction. Teaching is a broader and more flexible concept than instruction. For example, while we readily speak of teaching someone to understand physics, to appreciate music, or to swim, there is an awkwardness about *instructing* someone to understand physics, to appreciate music, even to swim—almost as if we could order someone to understand or appreciate. We can, of course, order someone to swim or to study physics, for that matter; but that is not the same as instructing another person in how to do those things. With instruction it's the how-to that makes all the difference.[2]

Instruction is a deliberate effort to impart specific information, facilities, or skills for which equally specific means (sources of information, practice schedules, methods, or steps to be followed) are available. Instruction also carries imperative force to the effect, "Do this if you want to learn how to do that," for example, to calculate the location of Mars on a given date, to analyze harmonic structure, to swim faster. In other words, instruction tends to be task specific and prudentially imperative, that is to say, *authoritative* (not necessarily authoritarian) to the extent that it is reliable.[3]

While teaching involves a good deal of instruction in particular skills, it is not overall reducible to instruction. Teaching, by contrast, is often more oblique, inadvertent, or unawares than instruction and includes such indirect modes of influence as involuntary example or suggestion and, of course, dialogue.[4] For instance, it might be said that Socrates taught a generation of Athenians what it means to be philosophically reflective without implying that he gave *instruction* in "being philosophically reflective" or "public virtue," as the Sophists pretended to do. On the contrary, Socrates's troubling questions and personal example proved the greater influence even to the extent of his being accused of "corrupting the young"—a charge never laid against the Sophists.[5]

And that is the key to teaching: *influence*. While no sharp line can be drawn between teaching and instruction, teaching influences in often ineffable ways that go beyond the details of instruction in one or another specific task. In the language adopted earlier, teaching aims to shape the sensibilities—in the sense of vision and taste—along with (by instruction) the facilities and skills needed for professional activity.

Catching on by instruction, then, comes down to technical proficiency, the necessary "know-how" to do the job well. What we can reasonably expect from instruction is that we be well *trained* in the basic skills and techniques required for minimal competency. However, sheer technical proficiency, even high levels of it, do not a professional make. Musicians, for example, speak of "musicianship" as a kind of added value beyond technical proficiency. It's one thing to know the notes; quite another to know the music. Perhaps the worst critical insult that can be hurled at a musician is to declare his or her performance "technically perfect" while leaving it at that! One expects professionals in any field to display a degree of judgment that reaches quite beyond base technical proficiency.

Similarly, the planners of the Mandel program realized that technical proficiency in various research or administrative methods, as crucial as it may be, is insufficient for high responsibility in the field of education. Accordingly, they sought to embed such instruction and training generally within the larger context of a philosophic (meaning historical, analytic) vision, on the one hand, and guided practice leading on to real-life applications, on the other. As I interpret the program, this involves a good deal of catching on by example as a way of expanding one's experience. Teaching and learning by example take us deeper than does instruction into the realm of professional growth.

CATCHING ON BY EXAMPLE

Case studies are among the leading ways of teaching and learning by example. One of the many purposes of the case study method is to sharpen one's analytic and interpretive abilities from the ground up, as it were. By examining real-life situations and challenges at leisure, one is forced not only to apply what knowledge one already possesses but to draw out the lessons from the cases examined to future similar ones. A good case study poses a problem or series of problems for which there is no simple solution but rather several possible ones having different consequences that require the student to hold in balance several instrumental factors. In other words, a good case study can be an example of one or many things and seldom "speaks for itself."

Unlike direct instruction or following explicit rules and directions, case analysis requires one to *see* the problem and come up with one or more solutions in what educators are fond of calling "the discovery method." This is not to deny that following instructions also requires interpretive effort on the part of the learner. It certainly does; for instruction of the "tell-and-do" variety can be very complex as, for example, in music instruction or training in the use of new computer software. Rather, the real difference is that an even greater interpretive effort involving observation, the assessment of evidence, and judgment is required to learn from cases or examples where no "rule of thumb" is provided. Hints and clues are one thing, rules and directions quite another; and it is a mistake—indeed, a hindrance to one's development—to demand that all of one's training in a given field be of the tell-and-do kind. The aim of any fully developed training program is to produce practitioners of flexible, autonomous judgment, not mere followers of preestablished routines.

While that *aim* is readily acknowledged among corporate trainers, for instance, my own consulting experience suggests that much confusion attends how to achieve it. The central confusion, as I see it, is the wish to discover or to devise yet another "bag of tricks" (rules and routines) for what at root is not a matter of routine. A certain dread of the unspecifiable seems to propel some individuals and institutions into a quixotic quest for a *technology* of expertise from top to bottom. That is a bit like trying to teach musicianship (or creativity or discovery, for that matter) as if it were just another facility to be mastered on a plane with running scales. The growth of professional judgment in virtually any domain proceeds along rather more devious routes. Learning by example is one of those routes.

Now, examples, like instructions, come in many forms and symbolic guises and serve quite different cognitive purposes. Case studies of the kind described are *simulations* that approximate in varying ways and degrees the real thing. Flight simulators, role-playing as in psychodramas or staged parliamentary proceedings, facsimilies of the Magna Carta or of diamonds ("stage jewelry"), even fictional maps of the Land of Lilliput or film "special effects" such as the dinosaurs in *Jurassic Park*—all give an *as if* experience or appearance of the real thing that escapes the risks, perhaps also the limitations, of everyday reality.[6]

A *sample*, by contrast, is a typical real instance like a tailor's cloth swatch or mineral sample. The signal for a sample or typical instance of something is usually a request or prefatory phrase to the effect, "Could you give a demonstration [illustration, example] of _____ ?" "For example . . ." "To illustrate . . ." "To demonstrate . . ." Providing samples (examples in that sense of the word) is the core of "show-and-tell" pedagogy. We may ignore the vagrant relations among samples, demonstrations, and illustrations in favor of a central feature of them all: their *typicality*.[7] If the objective is to show someone how to identify a certain plant, say, poison ivy, one selects samples that represent the range of properties of poison ivy, including several that are neither too "perfect" nor marginal, in order to get across the different appearances of the plant: its seasonal variations, locales, and differences from other similar plants.

An *exemplar* is also a sample but not a typical one. Rather, an exemplar is drawn from that end of the scale of samples that represent the very best or perfect-as-can-be *ideal* realization. Exemplars set a standard or ideal for the learner in either of two ways: First are those exemplars that establish an ideal in the sense of *fixing* it, like the standard yard, the orchestral "A" tuning pitch, or the printmaker's *bon à tirer*, which sets the standard for all prints made from the same plate or block; second are those exemplars that pursue, more than establish, an ideal by *furthering* it, like a new scientific discovery or theory, a definitive musical performance, a world record at 800 meters, or even a better mousetrap or other invention. The former we may think of as "closed" and the latter as "open" exemplars.[8]

Open exemplars are open-ended in ways that allow for indefinite further development even as they establish a new high point of achievement. Newton's mechanics were no less exemplary for their time than Einstein's quantum mechanics for our own. Both pointed toward new directions in physics yet unrealized. Similarly, Solti's Beethoven is no less exemplary an interpretation than von Karajan's or Bernstein's just for being different from the other two. Indeed, their divergences mark their achievements. Each conductor, following his own vision, discovers new depths of technical and expressive nuance in the Beethoven symphonies.

On the other hand, we should not assume that exemplars as such are *superior* among examples to samples for pedagogical purposes. Both serve different purposes in learning. Samples give us the whole (typical) range of a given phenomenon, whereas exemplars, whether open or closed, focus on one end of that range. Generally speaking, particular facilities like typing, running scales, or lifting weights are learned by reference to samples and closed exemplars where the differences between "right" and "wrong" ways of doing things are relatively straightforward; whereas advanced skills involving judgment and choice take the grayer measure of progress by reference to open exemplars. Critical assessment, not only of one's approximation to the standard thus set but of the standard itself, never ceases where an open exemplar is in force.[9] With open exemplars, it's more a matter of expanding the frontiers than of hitting the mark.

Finally, we come to *models* in the sense of scaled-up or scaled-down designs of structure, pattern, or function.[10] Like simulations but unlike samples and exemplars, models may be "realistic" without being real. The architect's cardboard model of a building, the physician's plastic breakaway model of the heart, the auto engineer's clay model of a new car design—each selects certain properties of the real thing for study and exhibition while ignoring others such as exact size, materials, or function. Models are in effect diagrams, often in two or three dimensions, with working parts. Their special instructional power lies in drawing "showing" and "telling" together in a single, complex symbolic representation.[11] A model directs our attention to certain aspects of design while showing them to us.

As found and used, simulations, samples, exemplars, and models are hardly distinct, unambiguous, or mutually exclusive. A sample of gold or cloth could well be exemplary. A "model student" could be either typical or exemplary; and a flight simulator is sometimes described as a "mock-up" or full-scale model of a cockpit. Nonetheless, what they all have in common from the standpoint of the learner is the necessity of proper *interpretation*. One must learn to what and where to attend in the examples proffered in order to learn from them; for nothing is given by example that cannot be taken (correctly) or mistaken. It would be a mistake, for instance, to dwell on the materials of the physician's heart model unless, of course, one is more interested in how such models are made than in what they tell us about the functions of the heart.

The latter point is germane to the variety of instructional uses to which examples can be put. What makes examples of any kind "good" or "bad" is how well they serve their cognitive purposes, and that in turn depends on the interests and purposes of teachers and learners alike. Examples of all kinds may exhibit or exemplify[12] any of the properties they actually possess. It's the learner's job to figure out which of them count for the purposes at hand and in what ways. If a single good example "says" more than a thousand words, it is only because one understands in principle what such a thousand words might be about. The thousands of words expended in case analyses have precisely that objective: to get the learner to see for himself or herself what the example in all its complexity has to teach us.

Where that understanding gets derailed or misdirected for lack of guidance, particularly in the area of *personal* example (taking someone as an exemplar), the results can be limiting at best or disastrous at worst. Novices at any difficult undertaking are notorious for picking up on irrelevant details, like Wittgenstein's sycophantic students mentioned earlier.[13] Many an aspiring artist, intellectual, politician, or business entrepreneur has been hobbled by the persons they seek to imitate. The people or personal traits you admire—those whom you would emulate—is something of a measure of your strategic and moral vision. Which brings me to the liabilities and strengths of imitation as a way of catching on.

CATCHING ON BY IMITATION

Imitating the manner, style, or methods of those we admire is an especially powerful way of learning by example. As children, we worshipfully imitate our elders' behavior from speech patterns to gait to their emotional attitudes, consciously and unconsciously. But, you might ask, should we not as adult learners put aside the slavish copycat behavior of children? To which I reply, Can you? Should you? and At what cost?

Can you? There is so much that we pick up by imitating others from childhood on that I rather doubt it can be avoided. Should you? Not if practice and drill play any part in your learning experience, which, inevitably, they must. Deliberate, *informed* imitation is a regular ingredient of most practice regimens. At what cost? The cost of eliminating imitation from our learning experiences would be, at the very least, most of the routine facilities and skills we need to survive personally and professionally. Not all imitation is slavish, unreflective, or sycophantic.

So why does imitation as a mode of learning from the example of others sometimes appear so disreputable? We need go no further than the dictionary to discover why. Besides being the sincerest form of flattery, imitation is also described in *The Concise Oxford Dictionary* as "following model or example (of); counterfeit." Right there, from the verb to the noun, lies the guilt by association, from imitating an example to producing or becoming a counterfeit, a "cheap imitation," as we say.[14] Therein also lies the connection between imitation and the exemplars we choose to be our guides. I recall a lecture by American soprano Phyllis Curtin in which she facetiously bemoaned the advent of the phonograph for its sometimes negative influence on young singers. "Down the corridors of practice rooms I hear a second hand Fischer-Dieskau here, a third hand Sutherland there—before they have even *begun* to find their own voices!"[15]

True enough, imitation has its liabilities.[16] But there is another side to the story, what elsewhere I called "the *striving* for perfection . . . the effort that goes into trying to 'live up to' our exemplars and the measures we take of our successes or failures. Such measures, to whatever extent 'given' in the exemplars, are taken in (absorbed) by ourselves with varying degrees of accuracy, sensitivity, vision, and diligence. We stand or fall as learners by the ways we aspire to the things we imitate and admire."[17] The emphasis here is upon the *ways* we aspire to the things we imitate and admire; for, as noted, not all imitation is slavish. To be *influenced* by the exemplary performances of others is one thing; to become a counterfeit clone of them is quite another, and there is plenty of ground between those extremes for autonomous development.

The secret for avoiding clonelike conformity either to the example of another person or to the established practices of one's chosen field or discipline is the exercise of conscientiousness and care, which, as John Passmore reminds us, "may not be the most fascinating of virtues, but virtues they are."[18] By exercising conscientiousness and care, we avoid soppy sentimentality as well as numbing conformity to precedent. And by them we may actually free our imaginations to convert an empty dream without means into reality.

How might this work in an actual case? British novelist Kingsley Amis describes his own beginnings as a writer:

> According to me, all writing is and should be to some extent a process of imitation; you like reading, you read a lot in general, you find yourself attracted to a particular subdivision of literature, you read that kind intensively, you reach a stage where you begin to think perhaps you can contribute something of that kind yourself. That is probably what is meant by a tradition; it was certainly what got me started on writing in the distant past.[19]

Here we see the other (positive) side of imitation where, through a combination of spontaneous attraction, immersion in a task or genre, and blatant imitation, one may find one's own "voice" as a singer, writer, politician, or corporate executive. Well, all right, so it happens that imitation is not all bad as a learning strategy, that it may even lead us on in the most beneficial ways. But *how* does it happen?

The answer to that question, I believe, has (at least) two parts. The first part has to do with making a commitment; that is, not only identifying what is involved in the task but also identifying *with* it—of taking the pros and cons of the task within oneself in the form of an "inner dialogue." We begin to see ourselves in the role, to feel our way into it by comparison to the behavior (performances, style, or tactics) of others.[20] At that stage the wish to find a way usually comes from imitating the ways of others. But how do we get beyond that stage? That brings me to the second part of the answer to the original question on how imitation can be beneficial.

Like any dialogue, the inner dialogue that I hold to be at the heart of deliberate imitation[21] gets more interesting as it *extrapolates* from the known and accepted to the unknown and experimental, even controversial. This is especially so regarding our attachment to open exemplars as models of judgment and comportment, whether they be persons whose style and abilities we admire or precedents that seem to us to define the undertaking to which we aspire. As we get better at something, we find our own way. To a lesser degree the same observation applies to closed exemplars, inasmuch as innovations in training methods for routine athletic, artistic, or work skills are commonplace.

Extrapolation from received ideals or practices becomes increasingly pertinent to professional growth, however, where such ideals engage our sensibilities and independent judgment in ever-changing circumstances. A primary benefit of that engagement, of the inner dialogue with our exemplars, is the ability to adapt our dreams and ideals to reality. Franklin D. Roosevelt, for example, greatly admired the international vision of Woodrow Wilson (in whose administration he served as Assistant Secretary of the Navy), particularly Wilson's attempts to establish a League of Nations. FDR in fact coined the phrase "United Nations" in 1942 first to describe the coalition of twenty-six Allied countries waging war against the Axis countries of Germany, Italy, and Japan.[22] He was determined, nonetheless, to avoid what he perceived to be Wilson's major foreign policy failures after World War I, namely, "to take sufficient steps to make certain that the Allied coalition would continue in the postwar era, and, most importantly, [Wilson's failure] to bring about a genuine understanding with the U.S.S.R."[23]

There are two stages of FDR's extrapolation from his mentor's vision notable here: first, his perception of Wilson's mistakes; and second, his pragmatic plan for corrective measures to be taken after World War II. It does not matter for our purposes that part of his plan succeeded (retention of the Allied coalition) and part of it failed (the rapprochement with the U.S.S.R.). What matters is that FDR reconstructed Wilson's design for a League of Nations in terms of the political realities of a new postwar era. He was no slave to his predecessor's ideals. He sought not to replicate Wilson's political vision but to further it.

At more mundane levels, imitation as an ingredient of practice and drill may acquire the perspective of the larger tasks and disciplines they serve; so there is nothing *inherently* opposed to the spirit of inquiry and discovery in the activity of imitation. Viewed in that spirit, routines and procedures learned by imitation invite extrapolation to the unknown. Even more do open exemplars (some great athletic or artistic achievement, for example) provide a sense of direction, pointing the learner beyond the done thing. Imitation, ranging from its replicative to its more influential forms, has as much to show us as our backgrounds and experience enable us to see.[24]

Often, we need a mentor or "coach" to nudge us along in the right directions, someone to apprentice us, as it were, in order to avoid the twin liabilities of bovine conformity and failure to learn from our own and others' mistakes. FDR, incidentally, had two quite different mentors early in his career: the badgering Louis Howe in domestic politics and the visionary Woodrow Wilson in foreign affairs.[25] Mentors provide vital guidance along the stages of catching on to the realities of the tasks before us. So I shall conclude this chapter with a brief look at apprenticeship relations.

CATCHING ON BY APPRENTICESHIP

A mentor could be an instructor, a teacher (in the broader sense), a friend or colleague, a parent, or a professional superior. Generally speaking, a mentor is someone from whom we learn *in medias res*, that is, in close proximity to the work we have undertaken. Which is why I spoke of apprenticeship *relations* just now: to underscore the fact that the mentor and the apprentice have a relationship rooted in the tasks at hand.

The contemporary social science literature prefers the terms mentor-protégé to the traditional master-apprentice terminology,[26] perhaps to avoid the narrower, crafts- and trades-centered connotations of the latter. I will drop the term *master* while retaining *mentor* and use the terms *apprentice* and *protégé* interchangeably.

Apprenticeship differs from learning by imitation or from exemplars at a distance, so to speak, by the mentor's *intervening* to make useful corrections or suggestions even if, at the time, the mentor's criticisms may appear negative or harsh. American football coach Vince Lombardi, for example, was less liked than respected by his players for his tough treatment of them. Ballet masters and voice coaches are notorious for their dictatorial tendencies. Nor are CEOs noted for conspicuous charity toward those whom they have taken under their wings. After all, they want results. So it is not necessary for an effective mentor-protégé relation to be a friendly one. It may well be so, but what sustains the relation is its reliability as a guide to improved performance. Once that reliability is undermined, the relation, however friendly, ceases to have its educative function.

What is necessary, besides the reliability of the guidance given, is that the apprentice *accept* the guidance for its worth, that he or she see it not as a personal attack (even if sometimes it is) but as an opportunity to learn something useful. It's important to emphasize the cognitive base of the mentor-protégé relation to compensate for the near-worshipful language in which such relations are often enshrouded. "I owe everything I know to my teacher." "My boss was the most wonderful person I have ever known." Or consider this encomium: "His persuasiveness, the peculiar magic of his by no means pleasant voice... the seductive simplicity with which he attacked the complexity of our problems—all fascinated me. . . . He had taken hold of me before I grasped what was happening." These are the words of Albert Speer on his political mentor, Adolf Hitler.[27]

Hero worship aside, the cognitive base of mentor-protégé relations is fundamental. What's the point of attaching yourself to someone professionally if not to learn something? It is unnecessary, however, that the mentor see himself or herself in that role as such. Acceptance of the role may or may not be explicitly acknowledged. Louis Howe's mentoring of FDR in the latter's early career was explicitly acknowledged by both men then and later; Wilson's mentoring was more tacit than explicit. It is only necessary that the mentor *play* that role relative to the protégé's interests. In other words, mentors tend to be chosen by their protégés rather than being officially or self-appointed, except in what might be called formally instructive situations such as schools, training programs, or private study (where, incidentally, the word *apprentice* is more likely to be used).

To put it another way, mentor-protégé relations tend on the whole to be rather more *collegial* than formal, more *collaborative* than teacher/student–like unless otherwise stipulated. The key to such relations is mutual reflection upon the protégé's (and sometimes the mentor's) successes and failures. It is as if the protégé were engaged in a continuing "open lesson" of a sort familiar to artists and musicians.[28] Inherited from more formal, instructional modes of learning is the protégé's deference to the mentor's superior knowledge, judgment, or vision. Without that, no such relationship can survive.

Discounting emotional and personality factors, such deference ideally rests on the cognitive base of the relationship: namely, the reliability of the advice and the assessments proffered. In the normal course of events, one may outgrow one's mentors to become friends, colleagues, rivals, or even enemies. Al Smith, whom FDR admired, whom he succeeded as Governor of New York, and whom he thrice nominated for the presidency, eventually became one of FDR's most bitter critics and opponents when FDR ceased to heed his advice. Conversely, protégés may go on to become mentors themselves to the next generation, as a number of New Deal politicians from Adlai Stevenson to Lyndon Johnson claimed FDR to have been to them.[29] The shifting sands of careers in the making create new learning patterns and alliances even as they undo old ones all along the way.

In a weak, metaphoric sense, anyone in a directive role becomes a model (meaning exemplar) and hence "mentor" just by occupying the role and exemplifying certain attitudes and behavior—even to the extent of being a model of how *not* to do the job. In a stronger sense, mentoring goes beyond mere modeling behavior to offer deliberate guidance. The person in authority becomes consciously aware of being an example to others.

A mentor on the job, as contrasted with someone whose primary job is giving instruction, assumes a double role that involves instructional intent, by whatever means, along with directive performance at the job. Given those formidable demands, little wonder that it takes great confidence and proven achievement for anyone to take up the role of mentor in such circumstances deliberately. Little wonder, too, that protégés more often choose their mentors rather than the reverse, usually on the basis of *perceived* success.[30]

An especially poignant kind of mentorship sometimes arises from failure, as, for example, when a failed candidate for high office or instigator of an unsuccessful reform lends the benefit of his experience to one more likely to succeed. Initially, Al Smith took custodial pride in boosting FDR's rising star, until, that is, the younger man ceased to heed his advice, prompting a bitter estrangement between the two men.[31] Thus do the sands shift in real life; which brings me to a final observation about catching on by apprenticeship in situations that are not formally instructional.

One may find, one may choose a mentor, seek that person's advice and counsel; or conversely, one may choose a protégé virtually anywhere. But contrary to some students of mentorship in the workplace,[32] I am skeptical of attempts to legislate or institutionalize such relations as catalysts to professional development. I am distinguishing, of course, training programs like that of the Mandel Institute where provisions for mentor-protégé relations are built into the program from those situations where they tend to occur spontaneously, as it were, in the midst of other concerns. What prompts someone to become a surrogate "parent," "big brother," or "big sister" in often competitive circumstances defies regulation. As mentioned earlier, such relations are typically formed out of mutual admiration—of perceived "success," on the part of the protégé, or "potential," on the part of the mentor.

Artists, artisans, and athletes, not to mention politicians, have long understood the precariousness and volatility of such relationships and value them when and where they naturally occur; but equally, they know enough to *let* them occur without trying to legislate them.[33] For these and other reasons, I suspect that attempts to assign mentor-protégé roles in the workplace are fundamentally misguided, except, of course, where employees take on extra instructional duties as a recognized part of the job like in many corporate training programs. I further suspect that such attempts are yet another manifestation of the impulse to codify and regularize what more often occurs by serendipity than design—like trying to teach professional judgment as if it were just another technical skill.

Work is not school, and catching on to the job takes many forms, as we have seen. The hierarchies of trades, businesses, corporations, and industries are fertile ground for the growth of mentor-protégé relations, and they are well deserving of extensive study; but such work-a-day hierarchies are not structured around learning as a goal (like schools and colleges) so much as profits, efficient performance, and output. The delivery of goods and services for a fair price shifts the priorities of learning onto an almost exclusively utilitarian plane, as Theo from earlier chapters quickly discovered. That is not an environment in which you can safely expect, as a matter of course, your peers and superiors to be "teachers" in any but the most cursory ways. While there is much to learn and many ways of learning it in any complex field or occupation, once you exchange a tuition bill for a paycheck, the responsibility for catching on becomes largely your own.

SUMMARY

I opened this chapter by noting that the experience of catching on to any new field or occupation proceeds in a variety of modes and rhythms, some of which involve teaching and direct instruction but just as many that do not. Accordingly, our reasonable expectations and experiences will vary with the mode of presentation.

From instruction we may expect to become well trained in whatever technical skills are required. I observed in passing that teaching as such is less task and method specific than training. Teaching reaches beyond technical proficiency to encompass a good deal of *in*direction, suggestion, and other inchoate influences. In addition, teaching places a premium on dialogue in a way that allows greater autonomy to the learner. As the broader concept, teaching includes instruction, and both make liberal use of examples.

Learning by example turns out to be rather more complex than just catching on to the examples and illustrations offered in show-and-tell pedagogy. Examples come in several forms: samples, simulations (or facsimilies), exemplars (open and closed), and models of many different types (including slippery metaphoric uses of the term). Each serves a different, if sometimes overlapping, cognitive purpose from the others, ranging from giving the appearance of reality to presenting bits of reality itself. What they all require of the learner, however, is greater interpretive effort to grasp their meaning and significance than merely doing as one is told as in following orders or instructions. In effect, examples of whatever kind do not "speak for themselves" so much as challenge and develop our observational, analytical, and evaluative powers.

I went on to argue that imitation as yet another way of learning by example and catching on is a regular ingredient of learning at all levels from drill to learning from the example of others' accomplishments. Rather than resulting in "counterfeit" or copycat behavior—always a liability—imitation, when coupled with commitment *and* discrimination, can, and frequently does, lead on by extrapolation to new discoveries and insights.

By way of filling in the picture of learning from the example and advice of others, I briefly reconnoitered the complexities of mentor-protégé relations in both formal and informal instructional settings. Acknowledging the personality factors that give such relations their rise or fall, I emphasized their cognitive base in the reliability of the examples provided and advice given. I also stressed the collegial nature of apprenticeship relations in the workplace while warning against the *expectation* that colleagues be teachers in any formal sense. Despite their frequency and obvious value to the novice, mentor-protégé relations occur more by happy chance than by design in the midst of the day-to-day demands of work.

Whatever their similarities and connections, school and work, I suggested, have quite different hierarchies and goals. Those differences, in turn, entail a shift from shared responsibility for one's development as occurs in school to a responsibility that increasingly devolves to oneself on the job.

NOTES

1. Mandel Institute for Advanced Studies in Education (unpublished internal memorandum, Jerusalem, Israel, 24 April 1994).

2. See Howard, *LBAM*, p. 62. Instruction is a prismatic concept, many facets of which are omitted here. For a fuller analysis, see ibid., chap. 5.

3. Ibid., p. 37.

4. Ibid., p. 62.

5. John Burnet, ed., *Plato's Euthyphro, Apology of Socrates, and Crito* (Oxford: Clarendon Press, 1977).

6. Howard, *LBAM*, pp. 116–19.

7. Ibid., p. 116.

8. Ibid., p. 120.

9. Ibid.

10. I am well aware of the many different meanings attached to the word *model* from mathematical models to fashion models. For simplicity's sake, I shall ignore most of them here. See Max Black, *Models and Metaphors* (Ithaca: Cornell University Press, 1962), for an excellent discussion.

11. Howard, *LBAM*, p. 118.

12. For a technical account of exemplification as a special type of symbolic reference undergirding examples of all kinds, see Howard, *LBAM*, pp. 111–15; Howard, *WA*, pp. 100–106; Nelson Goodman, *Languages of Art: An Approach to a Theory of Symbols* (Indianapolis: Hackett, 1972), p. 53f; and Nelson Goodman, *Ways of World Making* (Indianapolis: Hackett, 1978), p. 63f.

13. See Chapter 2, p. 43.

14. The Concise Oxford Dictionary 9th ed., s.v. "imitation"; see also Howard, *LBAM*, pp. 121–22.

15. Phyllis Curtin, "The Artist's Need to Teach" (talk delivered at the Harvard Graduate School of Education under the auspices of the Philosophy of Education Research Center, Cambridge, 16 November 1988).

16. Including some not mentioned herein such as perfectionism and "premature satisfaction." See Howard, *LBAM*, p. 124.

17. Ibid., p. 123.

18. John Passmore, *The Philosophy of Teaching* (Cambridge: Harvard University Press, 1980), p. 187; see also Howard, *LBAM*, pp. 123–24.

19. Kingsley Amis, *The Crime of the Century* (London and Melbourne: J. M. Dent & Sons, 1987), p. vi.

20. Howard, *LBAM*, p. 121.

21. Much of our imitative behavior is involuntary or nondeliberative such as a first accent, certain physical mannerisms, or whether one eats with a fork in the left or the right hand. That's what I mean by things we "pick up."

22. Nathan Miller, *F.D.R.: An Intimate History* (New York: Doubleday, 1983), p. 485.

23. Ibid., p. 481.

24. Howard, *LBAM*, p. 127.

25. Miller, *F.D.R.*, pp. 82–101.

26. Eliza Collins and Patricia Scott, "Everyone Who Makes It Has a Mentor," *Harvard Business Review* (July-August 1978): 89–101;

Kathryn M. Moore, "The Role of Mentors in Developing Leaders for Academe," in *Contemporary Issues in Leadership,* eds. William E. Rosenback and Robert L. Taylor (Boulder: Westview Press, 1984); Gerald Roche, "Much Ado about Mentors," *Harvard Business Review* (January 1979): 14–28; Eileen C. Shapiro, Florence P. Haseltine, and Mary P. Rose, "Moving Up: Models, Mentors, and the Patron System," *Sloan Management Review* (Spring 1978): 51–58; Jeanne J. Speizer, "Role Models, Mentors, and Sponsors: The Elusive Concepts," *Signs* (Summer 1981): 691–712.

27. Speer, *Inside the Third Reich*, p. 18.

28. Howard, *LBAM*, chap. 2.

29. See Miller, *F.D.R.*, chaps. 12 and 13, for an interesting account of the complicated mentorings and rivalries among FDR's associates.

30. See Howard and Scheffler, *WEL*, chap. 6.

31. Miller, *F.D.R.*, chap. 12.

32. Especially Moore, "The Role of Mentors"; and Collins and Scott, "Everyone Who Makes It Has a Mentor."

33. Howard and Scheffler, *WEL*, p. 13.

CHAPTER FOUR
GETTING IT TOGETHER

LEARNING ON BORROWED INTEREST

"There is, in fact, no greater school of effort than the steady struggle to attend to immediately repulsive or difficult objects of thought which have grown to interest us through their association as means, with some remote ideal end."[1] In making that pronouncement to teachers needing to engage their pupils' attention, James also spoke directly to the heart of all learning that is utilitarian in nature. Who would take an *intrinsic* interest in running scales, mending fishing nets, or underwriting insurance claims except as they have a certain "borrowed interest"[2] accruing to their remoter ends?

So much of what we need to navigate ordinary and professional life is sheer drudgery taken by itself, from brushing one's teeth or doing the laundry to attending sales meetings. If we were not acutely aware of what such activities are *for*, we would hardly find them compelling as necessities or as interests. Who would aspire to carrying out the trash as an end in itself? Yet if we didn't do it from time to time, we should be mightily inconvenienced by the mounting pile of rubbish around us. The borrowed interest in trash removal is in seeing it off to its proper destiny in the dump.

Of course, the remoter the ends, the vaguer their connection to the means of their realization, the more difficult it is to generate borrowed interest in those means. Means and their ends are ever in danger of becoming estranged. That estrangement, incidentally, is the origin of parental admonitions to the effect, "You'll thank me later on when . . ." or, "One day you will realize the value of this" and other promissory notes utterly lost on insouciant youth unable or unwilling to see the connection. It is also the origin of that hedonic attitude toward life and work that eschews consequences or the investment of time and effort in any but immediately pleasing or spontaneous activities. In the words of a well-known beer commercial, "Go for the gusto!" Gusto is neither borrowed nor deferred; it is here and now. Nor is it in any need of "schooling." The ecstatic joy of white-water rafting or heeling over in a stiff ocean breeze is instantly apparent on the faces of those depicted in the television and magazine advertisements (conveniently ignoring the considerable planning and training that go into rafting or sailing). It is as if you had only to reach out, now, for what you want. Long for the gusto of sailing or rafting? Get the same effect: Have a beer. Thus does the consumer life imitate Madison Avenue.

If time on blind task spells drudgery, blind pursuit of the buoyant moment may often spell waste, even tragedy. Douglas C. Kenney, progenitor of the *National Lampoon* and the manic film comedies *Animal House* and *Caddyshack*, was described by a Harvard contemporary as "a tub toy under sedation"; by a former *Lampoon* editor as "a big jerk, in the most affectionate way . . . iridescent."[3] By Kenney's own confession, "I'm the greatest comedy writer alive . . . no, I meant the biggest *asshole* alive."[4] Immensely talented, a multimillionaire by his late twenties, he continued to live hell-bent, leaving his new wife penniless after an affair with another woman, then dying in mysterious circumstances by a fall off a cliff on the Hawaiian island of Kauai in the summer of 1980. He was thirty-three.

Most jobs and occupations lie somewhere between the extremes of blind drudgery and the buoyant moment trading off borrowed interest for the schooling of effort, which is to say, by connecting means to their immediate or remoter ends. In the simplest terms, making that connection requires an answer to the question, Why am I doing this? Iterated over and over at various levels and stages of any long-term task undertaken, that question never seems to occur to the Douglas Kenneys—nor to those who reflexively reach for a beer at the suggestion of a television commercial. For example, if you are running scales on the piano, the answer might be as close to the cob as, "To learn the fingerings, the notes, and fluency of execution." Or the answer might be pitched at more distant goals such as, "To be able to play the music I like" or even, "To become a concert pianist."

So much may be obvious as a way of sustaining the interest borrowed from such goals and focusing our efforts; but the consequences of asking the question, Why am I doing this? are far-reaching and changeable over time and the growth of competence. Chief among those consequences is a continuation of the self-and-task reconstruction mentioned earlier in roughly two broad domains: first, in one's conception of the task itself—what you think it takes to do it well; and second, in the changing values that attend that growth.

AT THE APEX

Let's consider first the changes that occur in one's conception of the tasks at hand, as well as of the entire enterprise, as competency increases, be it at law, medicine, or boatbuilding. You might think of this metaphorically as the changing view as you climb the ladder of technical proficiency. Why am I doing this? reaches right to the top, as it were. The better you get at something, the broader and deeper the question becomes. The question expands your vision. More precisely, it represents an expansion of *strategic vision* of the kind discussed earlier.[5] Such vision, however, is earned gradually by attending to the habits, facilities, and critical skills that comprise technical proficiency and set performance standards. For convenience, we may think of performance standards as *internal* to the field or occupation taken up—as emerging from the field itself—as contrasted with the moral standards that govern our behavior overall. The latter, of course, enter into every aspect of life, including professional conduct, but in rather different ways, as we shall see.

Technical proficiency concerns both the *ideas* and the *ideals* of anything we consider worth learning, that is, both "how to" and "how well." Neither is static. For example, the very idea of what is involved in becoming, say, a doctor changes dramatically from that first fantasy of oneself in a white lab coat, stethoscope dangling from the breast pocket, to exposure to the rigors of medical school. Physiology, biochemistry, anatomy, long hours in the laboratory, internships, all loom before the aspirant to a medical career. Considerable borrowed interest parlayed across a wide variety of disciplines fuels progress toward getting the "feel" for medicine as a genuine occupation.

Merely acquiring skills, however, is insufficient to develop that feeling. We can all point to individuals of exceptional ability who either failed to live up to their original promise or just quit, for whatever reasons, in midstride. You might say, without irony, that their dreams did not match their abilities. Equally, you will recall others whose abilities did not match their dreams (the more common affliction); or yet others who, staggering at the start, picked up speed exponentially in their academic or professional growth. To be able is not necessarily to be willing, nor conversely. That's the difference between capability and motivation: The one says, You can. The other asks, But will you?

Beyond technical proficiency—and to a degree, even motivation—lie the shoals of personality and character that also affect the course of development. At a negative extreme, the essence of professional as of dramatic tragedy (in the classical sense of a "fatal flaw" of character) is where personality factors thwart ability, as in the case of Douglas Kenney's frenzied hedonistic mania. Such traits or tendencies to respond in ways conducive or nonconducive to success (or survival) are what philosophers are fond of calling *dispositions*.[6] A disposition toward thrift, for example, is not the same as the ability to balance a checkbook.[7] The disposition to practice medicine according to the Hippocratic oath is not the same as having advanced medical skills. Moreover, accountancy or medical skills are far easier to teach and to learn than the dispositions to use them in certain prescribed or preferred ways. Otherwise, corruption and incompetence would be unknown among financiers and physicians! Yet it is precisely the dispositions we acquire that enable us to connect effective means to ends in view, to put our skills to work in the service of an ideal or ambition.

So how do we acquire the "stuff" to do the job well? Can it be taught? Of course, many of our dispositions such as a tendency to introversion or extroversion are so deeply rooted in early personality development and biology as to be beyond teaching in any literal sense.[8] Most of our early dispositions are picked up willy-nilly from family, teachers, and associates, whereas others may be deliberately cultivated in a variety of ways. To the question whether the latter can be directly taught,

> I am inclined here to take the Socratic way out and say that they cannot be taught, not because they aren't learnt somehow, nor because they are unspecifiable, but because they have to be felt and absorbed as *aspirations* as well as known. That is the "aesthetic" face of all sustained learning and inquiry: the personal thrill of achievement and growth under the aegis of an ideal. Not until *the* task becomes *mine* does it come alive in thought and action.[9]

If that is so, then how do we shape our aspirations, acquire the ideals and standards of high-level performance? If dispositions are not taught, at least, not in the sense in which skills are taught, how do we learn them? The quick answer is: in so many ways, from so many sources, that it is a hopeless task to sort them all out. Still, I think there are three notable routes to identifying with a quest and acquiring the necessary borrowed interest to pursue it.[10]

First are our dreams of what we should like to become: a top-notch athlete, a firefighter, a doctor, lawyer, or opera singer. Such dreams are typically engendered by early exposure to exemplars of those endeavors: individuals (or their works) who appear to us to embody the best of the best, as well as exposure to the atmosphere and ethos of certain places: the grandeur of the Olympic stadium; the organized scramble in the fire station when the alarm bell rings; the intense concentration of the surgeon bent over the operating table; the measured drama of the courtroom; the music, voices, and colorful world of the opera stage. In a similar vein of kindred association, recall Kingsley Amis's discovery of his vocation as a novelist and critic through a combination of admiration and imitation of other writers in his youth. Opportunity, aptitude, instruction, not to mention such subtle personality traits as persistence, adaptability, and a tolerance for criticism also enter into the equation. How that equation factors out determines whether our dreams remain Mittyesque or are realized.

Second, dispositions just as often arise from the experience of instruction and experimentation with the unfamiliar, from the discovery of hidden abilities by trying something new. The thrill of discovery is bifocal pertaining as much to the Self as to the subject broached, self-centered only in the sudden realization, even at rudimentary levels, that this is something you *can do*. I recall a friend's amazement during his first tennis lesson several years ago upon realizing that he possessed a "natural" overhand serve, a maneuver others usually find difficult to master.

Surprise and elation at the dawning of new competencies is a powerful inducement (what psychologists call "positive reinforcement") to go on. As one corporate consultant put it to me, "The best way to find out where you want to go is to begin trying to get there." To which it might be added that trying new things is an equally good way to find out where you *don't* want to go. In that regard, the discovery of "hidden talent" is less a matter of unearthing the innately latent than of finding, through experimentation, the proper match between temperament and technique.

Finally, and most broadly, dispositions positive or negative are mostly learned by example in all the ways previously discussed: from the people we admire or loathe; from teachers and colleagues who embody in their actions and abilities what it is that we are striving for; from observing with increasing acuity the accomplishments or failures of others. Eventually, borrowed interest becomes self-sustaining when at last we learn to learn unassisted from the example of others, from the work itself undertaken, and from our own mistakes. In that way, even conspicuous failure (whether that of others or one's own) may become the occasion for critical reflection and self-instruction. In that way, too, the apprentice becomes one's own master.

Throughout that odyssey, imagination supports critical hindsight and foresight less as a matter of inspiration than of aspiration within a means-ends continuum linking technical skills to the propelling disposition to do well. We begin to see in the mind's eye how things *connect*. In effect, the entire conception of the task or job at hand deepens in interest and complexity and in the connections made among ideas and the world of their application. We also experience a corresponding sharpening of judgment as we approach the apex of our powers, which, if we are wise, alerts us to hazards as well as to opportunities unforeseen by others less experienced.

You can get an idea in miniature of that dual transformation of the Self-on-task by comparing what you knew (or thought you knew) about, say, economics from the first to the last day you were enrolled in a class on that subject. If the class was a success, you will have emerged not only better informed on economic matters, equipped with new analytical techniques, but with a strong sense of the limits of your knowledge and a disposition to further inquiry (whether or not you actually follow up on it).

Extrapolating from such small-scale experiences to the prospect of a *career* as an economist or a businessperson, it is easier to see what happens. The pure fantasy of earlier dreams is transformed into a strategic vision encompassing the nearest details to hand in relation to their farthest consequences and objectives. The effect is like a ship's captain bringing his vessel through shoals and storms to port. When the question, Why am I doing this? becomes jejune as regards your technical abilities and the disposition to deploy them as best you can, you will have "arrived." There is more to it than that, of course, but by that time, you shall be as much in control of your professional destiny as time and chance allow.

Like any long voyage, however, the growth of professional judgment is fraught with risk. As John Dewey reminds us, "Where there is reflection there is suspense."[11] Perhaps the first real *sense* of what scientific objectivity, evidential support, and honesty mean, not merely as logical abstractions but as personal values of the scientist, comes with the failure of a major experiment or cherished theory. Then the scientific investigator has a choice to make: to quit altogether; to gloss over or conceal the negative results (there have been many such cases of scientific fraud); or to revise his or her methods and thinking to suit the new contingencies. Only the latter is in the true spirit of scientific inquiry and honesty, which, after all, is as much a scientific as a moral virtue. That choice is a test of the character and standards, not merely of the technical skills, of the investigator.

In his *What Mad Pursuit*,[12] Francis Crick, the codiscoverer of the structure of the DNA molecule and a Nobel laureate, chronicles several such choice points in a long and distinguished career—including what to do after the apex of a major discovery has been reached. Throughout his account, he stresses the regulative values and ethos of the scientific enterprise absorbed over a lifetime. Indeed, Crick confesses to having had no teachers, as such, in his speciality; but by developing a nose for the "tractable problem" he was led to form many productive collaborations with other specialists (including James Watson with whom he shared the Nobel Prize) whose work complemented his own. A less courageous investigator might not have been so willing to expose his weakness alongside his strengths—or so likely to profit from the frank recognition of both.

COPING WITH WORK'S CHANGING VALUES

As the challenges of work change, so do you, and so do your values, not only those that emerge *out of* the work (in the form of performance standards) but also the value you *take in* the work, its practical and moral worth to you as a life's investment. In Aristotelian terms, your practical (moral) perspective changes in proportion to, if not directly with, a growth in productive knowledge. The question, Why am I doing this? is itself transformed from one of strategic vision to one of moral vision. In short, what do I owe myself and others?

For all the efforts of guidance counselors, parents, teachers, personnel advisors, and even headhunters and image makers to steer people in the right directions, to match people and positions properly, such advice tends to be ante facto, at best barely adequate to get you over the threshold from school to work or from one job to another. Thereafter, you are on your own for the most part in deciding what value to attach to the work you do.

In acute cases of disenchantment, the insights of a therapist may be required to untangle the skein of motives, stresses, ambitions, and values that come to clutter our minds in the midst of other preoccupations. A veritable welter of conflicting influences and interests besets the professional practitioner at every stage of his or her career.

One of the most fundamental conflicts concerns whether you seek influence or leadership. That is an especially acute problem for "intellectuals"—artists, scientists, scholars, thinkers of every stripe who seek after the truth or self-expression for its own sake. Leaders, by contrast, seek to marshal the talents and efforts of others in pursuit of a common goal.[13] The key to influence is no compromise. The key to leadership is the exact opposite: compromise. Which shall you serve? Can you serve both?

"The Leader," Garry Wills reminds us, "needs to understand followers far more than they need to understand him. This is the time-consuming aspect of leadership. It explains why great thinkers and artists are rarely the leaders of others (as opposed to influences on them)." In other words, "the great scientist does not *tailor* his view of, say, the atom to whatever audience he hopes to influence, as Lincoln trimmed and hedged on slavery in order to make people take small steps in the direction of facing the problem."[14] In much the same way, FDR trimmed and hedged on preparations for war in 1939–40 in order to give a reluctant Congress and public time to catch up to the reality of the threat.[15] By contrast, Picasso in May of 1937 finished perhaps his most famous painting, *Guernica*, to protest the German bombing of the historic Basque town of Guernica on 26 April of that year during the Spanish Civil War. Queried as to his political sympathies at the time, he replied, "In the panel on which I am working, which I shall call *Guernica*, and in all my recent works of art, I clearly express my abhorrence of the military caste which has sunk Spain in an ocean of pain and death."[16] No compromise there. The painting's influence on public opinion in Spain and abroad was enormous; but Picasso himself sought no political power, nor did he lead an army of followers against Franco.

The tension between influence and leadership as *values* increases with maturity and advancement in many fields. Scholars and research scientists, for example, are particularly apt to dismiss a colleague as "ruined for further serious work" when he or she aspires to an administrative position.[17] The presumption, often correct, is that the shift from the no-compromise pursuit of truth for its own sake, whatever its consequences, to the delicate arts of negotiation, persuasion, and compromise is irreversible. The same goes for those who popularize their own or others' works. Most professional philosophers, for instance, distinguish between the early "serious" Bertrand Russell of *Principia Mathematica* and the later, "activist" Russell of *Why I Am Not a Christian* and leader of nuclear protests. As Wills remarks, "It is hard to find an intellectual leader whose own deepest and creative work was carried on while he or she exercised leadership."[18] There are exceptions like Socrates, St. Augustine, and Voltaire, but they are rare.[19]

Because of the conflicting demands of scholarly influence and accomplishment versus administrative leadership, most academics nowadays make that choice early on in their careers—usually through involvement on committees where one may discover a liking or flair for administration. Increasingly, academic leaders are chosen from the ranks of those who studied administration in graduate schools of education or business.

For those who must make the choice later in their careers, however, the shift in values involved is a serious one fraught with Deweyan suspense. Perusing the works of a talented geologist recently, I learned from his former dean that he aspired to administration and so gave up research to take up a minor decanal post. Lacking the personal qualities, the so-called people skills, for such work, he has since drifted discontentedly from one low-level position to another. Listening to the details of this story, I could not but feel pity for a man so lacking in self-knowledge and moral vision as to sacrifice his own best interests (in both senses of the term).

On the other hand, careers may also have their rhythms and stages that readily accommodate shifts of focus or emphasis. A senior research scientist may feel a *responsibility* to use his hard-won influence in an administrative capacity to set future directions, coordinate the work of others, attract new talent to the field, and promote its work to the public, government, or funding agencies. Francis Crick, for example, temporarily assumed just such a leadership role as Acting President at the Salk Institute in California, putting his own work aside for a time. Similarly, the violinist Isaac Stern took over leadership in the campaign to save and restore Carnegie Hall in New York City. An early proponent of the National Council for the Arts, he continues an active performance and recording schedule at seventy-seven.[20] As in Crick's and Stern's cases, leadership may not be a sentence; it may only be for a term or special cause. In both instances, the shift from influence to leadership, whether permanent or temporary, was a natural evolution based on conspicuous achievement in their respective fields.

In some fields, however, conspicuous achievement is *equated* with the rise to leadership. The idea is that if you are really good at something, you shall become a leader at it. In politics, certain segments of corporate management, and law, the goal is not only to do the job well but to get elected or to win the top spot, to become CEO or a senior partner. Unlike scholarship or the arts (or even sport), where those of conspicuous achievement will often eschew administrative or other leadership posts in order to pursue their special interests, a rising young executive or military officer is *expected* to aspire to higher levels of leadership. As noted, a scholar or scientist may well lose influence or prestige in his or her field (unless already well established) by such aspirations. It is not at all uncommon to hear faculty say, So-and-so "abandoned the field" or "gave up serious work" to go into administration, so differently are the two realms perceived and valued, so differently are their *rewards* perceived and valued.

By contrast, it borders on hilarity to imagine one corporate executive saying of another, "She gave up serious work to accept a vice-presidency." Only rarely, and usually for extenuating reasons, would a corporate vice-president, a major in the army, or a junior partner in a law firm refuse promotion to the next rung of leadership. Moving up the ladder of *influence* in some fields, on the other hand, may actually require that you avoid the ingratiating, negotiating, agonistic compromises of leadership.

Another conflict of values that besets many young professionals is whether you live to work or work to live. In its starkest terms, the question is whether you will do whatever it takes to follow your bliss, including the sacrifice of material rewards, or whether you will do whatever work that maximizes those rewards. Another version: Will you do anything to realize your ambitions, or will you compromise those ambitions to support a certain lifestyle? Naturally, and reasonably, most of us seek work that is both satisfying in itself and materially rewarding; but the *tension* between living to work and working to live has a way of cropping up at awkward moments: for example, when, or if, you decide to get married; when the baby arrives; when you get that lucrative offer that requires uprooting and a change-of-career focus; or when it becomes clear that promotion and advancement depend on almost total dedication to time on task. The latter, especially, has become a pressing issue of our time.

I recall a television talk show from a few years back that dealt with prostitution at high corporate levels in America's major cities. One elegant, articulate, obviously well educated madam declared that the majority of her "clients" were rising young executives who had neither the time nor the desire to form "relationships." An evening's transient (and expensive) intimacy was their sole recreation. Otherwise, their lives revolved entirely around work.

Similarly, Felice N. Schwartz created an uproar among feminists' and women's groups several years ago with an article in the *Harvard Business Review*[21] in which she argued that "career-primary" women (or men, for that matter) who aspire to high corporate positions face such demands on their time and energies that normal family life may be impossible. Traditional marriages in which women took the major responsibility for child rearing and housekeeping made it easier for men to devote the bulk of their energies to work; but in the present climate of social change, men and women compete for the same professional prizes with fewer supports on the home front. In effect, Schwartz argues that the "have it all" ethos is grossly misleading to the majority of women aspirants to high position. Something has to give, and usually it is personal relationships, particularly those of a demanding sort such as children or disgruntled spouses. In Schwartz's words,

> Like many men, some women put their careers first. They are ready to make the same trade-offs traditionally made by the men who seek leadership positions. They make a career decision to put in extra hours, to make sacrifices in their personal lives, to make the most of every opportunity for professional development. For women, of course, this decision also requires that they remain single or at least childless or, if they do have children, that they be satisfied to have others raise them.[22]

Really, there is nothing new in this except that it now applies to ambitious women as much as to men with no "natural" division of labor to support either. So what is Schwartz's advice? Go for it if you are willing to accept the price, but recognize that there *is* a price. In other words, live to work. Otherwise, accept the fact that a sacrifice of ambition may be a condition of leading a more balanced life. For those nurtured on the "have it all" ethos, this is anathema. Personally, I have no advice on how to reconcile professional and private ambition where they conflict except to sound a note of warning: It could happen to you.

Work, like alcohol, can become addictive, altering in the value you attach to it to where it crowds out all other considerations over long exposure. Even leisure construed as "free time" (time off from work) comes to be seen in the image of time on task, as time to be *filled* in the relentless pursuit of pleasurable activities.[23] When, in the words of actress Bette Davis, you begin to think, "Only work will never let you down,"[24] keep in mind the logical obverse of that statement: Everything and everybody else will.

There are people—geniuses and the obsessively ambitious— who live to work virtually from the start, often from childhood. There is a beauty and elegance in their single-minded commitment (and sometimes not a little ruthlessness) that is the envy of anyone seeking a vocation or calling in life. Such individuals, however, tend to stake out their claim to a given area or discipline, be it figure skating, physics, or the violin, fairly early in their development. As observed in an earlier chapter, their problems may (or may not) come later when their technical skills and judgment are discovered not to match the magnitude of their dreams.[25]

For most of us, our work ambitions tend to grow more slowly in the context of other life changes: choosing a major, graduating from school or college, getting married, finding a job, discovering new interests and talents. Which is to say, we are less *defined* than those of monocular vision by the personal value we place on a given job or occupation. With increasing definition of such value (finding what we want to do), we change in ways that affect all our other values, including moral values. Consider, for instance, the campus radical ten years down the pike. Now a stockbroker on Wall Street, she has dropped her leftist-leaning friends for a coterie of financial investors and consultants. The world of high finance has become *her* world. She rediscovers a rapport with her banker father that had been missing since early adolescence. Her taste in clothes, her social views and politics, and her outlook on marriage and family life have all changed in one way or another. The changes could just as well have gone in the opposite direction: from being a campus conservative to becoming a social activist, political lobbiest, and editor of a radical feminist magazine.

The point is not to predict, prescribe, still less to judge such volatile changes as can occur in early adulthood. You may pass through several jobs before finding your true work. That experience will itself wreak changes of attitude and expectations. Rather, the point is that the work you finally choose, or as we say, that "absorbs" you for longer periods of a lifetime, is less something your unchanging Self does than something you become in changing. The more you get into it, the more it gets into you. It becomes part of your identity. That includes the work's emergent values—its standards of rigor, performance, and comportment—as well as its worth to you as a means or as an end in itself. Not even Theo, who made the most of his challenges on a personal plane, could escape that existential predicament (I hesitate to say fate).

BURNOUT

"Burnout": The phrase connotes energy used up, momentum lost, an engine run to ruin. Applied to human affairs, the suggestion is of dissipated interest, lassitude, exhaustion, confusion, not to mention depression at the foregoing. Burnout takes many forms: dashed career ambitions, the blocked writer, the executive beaten down by the rat race, the athlete no longer able to compete at top form, the singer who has lost her voice, the CEO who cracks under the strain of a corporate takeover. Indeed, there are as many types of burnout as there are of failure. Failure need not spell burnout, but when combined with inability to cope, confusion about what one wants, who one is, and loss of self-esteem, it usually does.

Typically associated with middle age, with the so-called midlife crisis,[26] burnout can occur at any age after infancy and just as often accompanies success as failure. Peruse the biographies of child movie stars like Jackie Cooper or Shirley Temple.[27] Listen to the threnodies of Little Leaguers harassed by their fiercely competitive parents and coaches, or consider these words of novelist Graham Greene: "At this period I was not unhappy at school except that, when I was twelve and I was moved into the top junior form, I remained at the bottom of the class for a whole term and lost my confidence."[28] Obviously, he recovered not only from that humiliation but from chronic shyness to become one of the greatest writers of the century. But the point remains: Burnout can occur at any age.

As a professor, I am well acquainted with the symptoms in my students: a sickness to heart of the whole "academic game," inability to concentrate, a furtive wanderlust, excessive partying. Mindful of the gospel of relaxation,[29] I usually recommend taking a year or two off to travel, see the world, or work at something totally unrelated to their studies. Maniacally ambitious or overly protective parents seldom agree (who are, after all, part of the problem), but the wiser ones see the point.

As for the burnout of success, it goes something like this: "Well, I've made it. I did it. Is this all there is?" As George Bernard Shaw once remarked with his characteristic pith, "There are two tragedies in life. One is not to get your heart's desire. The other is to get it."[30] The problem with success is how to follow it up. What to do next. As Nancy Mayer, author of *The Male Mid-Life Crisis*, bluntly puts it in terms that now apply to women as well as men:

- What am I breaking my a___ for?
- Is this really all there is?
- What have I accomplished anyway?
- Why isn't it making me happier?
- And what the hell *would* make me happy?[31]

It's interesting to reflect on the fact that the same set of questions eventually confronts the unsuccessful and the successful, but for different reasons: the one because of a perceived shortfall in accomplishment, in a word, frustration; the other because of loss of a goal (by achieving it), in a word, letdown. One may feel let down by the reality of the achievement compared to the dream or, by the costs, the toll taken, to "make it."

Commenting on highly successful men in terms that now apply equally to both sexes, Mayer writes, "It is not a matter of how many rewards a man has gotten—money, status, power, or fame—but of the goodness of the fit between his life structure and his evolving self. A man may do very well in terms of reaching his goals, but find success hollow or bittersweet. The severity of his crisis depends on the extent to which he questions his life structure and feels a need to modify or change it."[32] Burnout of both kinds, whether that of success or of failure, requires a reassessment of aims and goals, as previously distinguished, in terms of the questions, Why am I doing this? Is it worth it? What next? Not easy questions to deal with from the depths of despair or ennui.

Many new Ph.D.s, for example, go through a period of post partum blues after finishing their doctoral dissertations. Having completed a major piece of research and writing under close scrutiny, often with many setbacks, revisions, and struggles with a thesis committee unable to agree among themselves, let alone with the candidate, on what shape the thesis should take—having survived all that, usually in penurious circumstances, nerves and old clothes frayed—they find themselves at the end exhausted, listless, aimless. Deprived of the *one* goal that was for several years the focus of their lives, they feel themselves at a loss what to do next even as the pressures mount to find employment. The accomplishment, once done, appears altogether underwhelming in significance. Classic burnout.

In the words of the old cliché, anticipation is greater than realization. Consider this testimony of one of Mayer's subjects, "Peter J.," a senior partner in a large accounting firm, millionaire, and author of two bestselling novels!

> Anytime I take on anything new I seem to have a marvelous time while I'm working, and then when I've *got* it I don't want it anymore. The real happiness is in the process of getting to it, but I haven't yet found out what you do when you get there. . . . You see, as soon as I hear the word "success," something sort of rebels. I don't consider that I've ever *had* success, really. I've managed to achieve certain limited goals, and get the rewards in terms of money, or in some situations, acclaim. And in that way I exceeded what I set out to get. But to me success has to be measured in terms of some sort of *internal* contentment. And that I have never had, and never will.[33]

Looking at this statement in terms of its logic reveals something of the speaker's *conceptual* orientation as well as his psychological difficulties. Note the recurrence of the words "get," "getting," "success"; the mention of "limited goals" and "acclaim"; the wistful reference to "internal contentment." Clearly, Peter J. is a man of remarkable strategic vision in the achievement of his goals. He knows how to "get there," to "make it." But what are his aims in the sense of objectives of inherent worth to him? Where are the values that permeate his cleverness in accomplishment? They are precisely what is lacking, and he *knows* it. The reference to "internal contentment" reveals as much. In other words, he has no answers to the questions, Why am I doing this? What do I owe myself?

Peter J. lacks moral vision of the kind that motivates and sustains our old friend Theo through his professional successes and failures. Theo knows what he wants, what he owes himself. He has a project that *is* his life, one that takes satisfaction in mastery of difficult subjects of inherent worth to him. His projects and goals never pale with achievement, for they never end and have intrinsic value beyond mere "getting" and worldly success. You might say that Theo understands devotion. Peter J. for all his accomplishments does not, and hence, internal contentment eludes him.

Innumerable psychological studies of burnout as an inevitable companion of maturity, especially of early middle age, explore the phenomenon in detail and make many recommendations for how to cope with it.[34] They tend, on the whole, to see burnout as linked to a certain *stage of life*, usually the years thirty-five to forty-five. My point, however, is that burnout can occur at virtually *any* age and, admittedly in rather different form, afflicts youngsters and students as much as their elders. The increasing incidence of teenage suicide, particularly among the affluent, is a poignant reminder that hopelessness and despair know no boundaries of age or station. Loss of *significance* is a frightful and constant hazard of life and rejuvenating it a constant challenge. "Getting it together" in school or on the job is never ending. As a gloss on that challenge, I can do no better than to leave you, as I began, with these words of William James:

> Wherever a process of life communicates an eagerness to him who lives it, there the life becomes genuinely significant. Sometimes the eagerness is more knit up with the motor activities, sometimes with the perceptions, sometimes with the imagination, sometimes with reflective thought. But, wherever it is found, there is the zest, the tingle, the excitement of reality; and there *is* "importance" in the only real and positive sense in which importance ever anywhere can be.[35]

SUMMARY

I began by considering the ways we "borrow interest" from our more distant goals to school our efforts to master skills, some of them full of drudgery taken by themselves, necessary to realize those goals. I suggested that keeping the question, Why am I doing this? before your mind's eye enables you to link means to their proximate as well as remoter ends. That in turn will help you to avoid the twin cul de sacs of blind drudgery and blind self-indulgence. Iterated over time and changing circumstances, the question, Why am I doing this? is a transforming one as regards both the tasks undertaken and the changing values that accompany the growth of competence.

As you get it together and approach the apex of your powers, you will also experience further changes in your strategic vision, not only in "how to" and "how well" (matters of technical proficiency) but in your dispositions to deploy your abilities in the service of one or another ideal (moral vision): material rewards, a certain way or standard of living, or devotion to an inherently valuable vocation. Factored into that equation will be aspects of personality and character that also strongly affect the outcome: how well you do *and* what it means to you to do it.

I expressed skepticism about dispositions being the direct result of teaching (like skills) at either the strategic or moral levels of outlook. They are, nonetheless, acquired subtly from various sources: mostly from early dreams, from experimentation and discovery of unexpected capabilities, and from the example of others and their works past and present. Imagination is a critical factor in this development, enabling you to cast your mind backward and forward across the field, to see its potential, and to forecast to some degree your place in it. That represents a growth of judgment through deepening exposure to the field's details and demands. Often, a significant setback or failure is the best measure of commitment to the values and costs of "making it."

Among the conflicts of value that beset professionals in some fields are the competing attractions (and rewards) of influence versus leadership. Influence, I argued, requires less compromise personally and professionally than leadership, the essence of which is compromise in enlisting the efforts of others toward a common goal. Another conflict is between the extremes of living to work (as in having an all-consuming vocation or driving ambition to make it at all costs) and working to live (to support a certain standard of living or balanced lifestyle). I noted in this connection the addictive tendency of work over time as it comes increasingly to form a part of one's personal identity: from being something one does to being what one *is*.

Ignoring that tendency toward absorption of the Self in work can, and often does, lead to burnout: exhaustion, frustration, and confusion about what it's all worth. Burnout, I argued, can accompany success ("Is this all there is?") as well as failure ("I didn't make it. Now what?") and can afflict people of all ages, not only the middle aged.

Finally, with James's help, I suggested that in the last analysis the *significance* of what you do lies less in external markers of success or failure, in money or status, than in its importance *for yourself*. That is, the personal estimate of the worth of your efforts derives from your moral vision (whatever it is), which also needs renewal from time to time.

NOTES

1. James, *Talks*, p. 56.

2. James's phrase; ibid., p. 55.

3. Craig Lambert, "The Life of the Party," *Harvard Magazine* (September-October, 1993): 36–45.

4. Ibid., p. 38.

5. Keep in mind also that we are circling the topic of learning for work from different angles and altitudes.

6. Ryle, *The Concept of Mind*, chap. 2; also Scheffler, *Conditions of Knowledge*, pp. 19–20.

7. The example is Scheffler's; see his *Conditions of Knowledge*, p. 19.

8. Jerome Kagan and Howard Moss, *Birth to Maturity: A Study in Psychological Development* (New York: Wiley, 1962); also see Ruth Mehrtens Galvin, "The Nature of Shyness," an update on Kagan's recent work, in *Harvard Magazine* (March-April 1992): 40–45.

9. Howard, *LBAM*, p. 18.

10. Ibid., pp. 18–19.

11. Dewey, "How We Think" (1910), in Jo Ann Boydston, ed., *The Middle Works of John Dewey 1910–1911*, vol. 6 (Carbondale: Southern Illinois University Press, 1985), p. 189.

12. Crick, *What Mad Pursuit*, chap. 2, "The Gossip Test," pp. 15–23.

13. Wills, *Certain Trumpets*, p. 17.

14. Ibid., p. 16.

15. Miller, *F.D.R.*, pp. 419–20.

16. Arianna Stassinopoulos Huffington, *Picasso, Creator and Destroyer* (New York: Avon Books, 1988), p. 232.

17. See Wills, *Certain Trumpets*, pp. 161–62.

18. Ibid., p. 162.

19. Wills's discussion of intellectual leadership versus influence is especially insightful and illuminating to those unaccustomed to drawing the distinction. Ibid., chap. 10.

20. Herbert Kupferberg, "Stern at Seventy," *Classical* (July 1990): 14–20.

21. Felice N. Schwartz, "Management Women and the New Facts of Life," *Harvard Business Review* (January-February 1989): 65–76.

22. Ibid., p. 69.

23. Howard and Scheffler, *WEL*, pp. 17–20.

24. Recalled from a television interview she gave several years ago.

25. See Chapter 1, p. 21.

26. Daniel J. Levinson, et al., *The Seasons of a Man's Life* (New York: Ballantine Books, 1978); also see Nancy Mayer, *The Male Mid-Life Crisis: Fresh Starts after Forty* (New York: Doubleday, 1978).

27. Shirley Temple, *Child Star: An Autobiography* (New York: McGraw-Hill, 1988).

28. Graham Greene, *A Sort of Life* (New York: Simon & Schuster, 1971), p. 64.

29. See Chapter 2, p. 35.

30. George Bernard Shaw, *Man and Superman* (1903), act 4.

31. Mayer, *The Male Mid-Life Crisis*, p. 3.

32. Ibid., p. 174.

33. Ibid., p. 164.

34. See, for example, the copious bibliographies of Levinson, et al., *The Seasons of a Man's Life*; and Mayer, *The Male Mid-Life Crisis*.

35. James, *Talks*, p. 115; italics his.

CHAPTER FIVE

TOUGHING OUT
THE REAL WORLD

"THE NEW, RUTHLESS ECONOMY"

In the 29 February 1996 issue of the *New York Review of Books*, there appears an article entitled "The New, Ruthless Economy" by Simon Head.[1] Correspondent for Great Britain's *Financial Times* and for the *New Statesman* in America, Head presents a rare, accessible overview of domestic and international economic trends affecting both manufacturing and service industries now and for the foreseeable future—everywhere. For anyone crossing the school/work divide, Head's article, not to mention the many books, studies, and public speeches he cites, lays bare some economic facts of contemporary life that any new graduate needs to know. To whet your appetite for "survival reading" in this area, I will summarize the gist of Head's article while throwing in further observations of others as well as some of my own.

Head opens his article by noting that despite economic growth unprecedented since the 1950s following the 1990–91 recession—including declining inflation, rising investments, and increasing productivity—the living standard of most Americans has stagnated, indeed has stagnated since the early 1970s (about the time of the OPEC oil crisis, I would say, when Theo lost his academic job). Increases in real wages have not kept pace with increases in productivity. "This is the first time in American postwar history," he says, "that the real wages of most workers have failed to increase during a recovery."[2] This is an extraordinary fact. In other words, while the gross national product (GNP) has gone up, worker earnings have gone down and unemployment is increasing. In past recoveries, worker earnings have routinely increased and unemployment decreased. In a speech to the George Washington University School of Business and Public Management, Robert Reich, U.S. Labor Secretary, described what the old social contract used to be:

> So long as the company earned healthy profits, employees could be assured of secure jobs with rising wages and benefits, and their communities could count on a steady tax base. When the economy turned sour, employees might be laid off for a time. But when the economy revived, the work would return.[3]

Not so anymore. What is happening? Head quotes Wall Street investment banker Felix Rohatyn:

> What is occurring is a huge transfer of wealth from lower skilled, middle-class American workers to the owners of capital assets and to a new technological aristocracy with a large element of compensation tied to stock values.[4]

In other words, the rich and technologically sophisticated are getting richer while the middle class, not just the poor, is getting poorer. The result is fear and anger for many blue- and white-collar employees with the added danger, in the words of Nobel laureate Robert Solow, of creating a society "which might turn mean and crabbed, limited in what it can do, worried about the future."[5] We are used to blue-collar layoffs and workers asserting themselves through union action—but highly educated M.B.A.s and senior executives running scared? That's something new. Why is it happening?

The answer can be given in two pregnant phrases: "information technology" combined with industrial "reengineering." It's the combination of the two that has brought about the situation Rohatyn describes. Reengineering is a corporate buzzword that has been bandied about since the mid-1980s reaching the level of a corporate mantra in the 1990s. While having a profound effect on the economy, it is, Head says, "a less grandiose activity than it sounds. The main task of the reengineer is to use information technology to streamline many of the more routine activities of business."[6]

How does this work? Let's take manufacturing first, then the service industries like banking, insurance, and communications. The reengineer's buzz phrase in manufacturing is "lean production." It's a mass production idea borrowed from the Japanese having three main requirements: "[P]roducts must be easy to assemble ('manufacturability'); workers must be less specialised in their skills ('flexibility of labour'); and stocks of inventory must be less costly to maintain (components arrive at the assembly plant 'just in time,' and so save on both warehousing and financing costs)."[7]

The first two requirements have the greatest impact on the workforce. Because the products (automobiles, electronics, machine tools) are easy to assemble, industrial corporations no longer need to maintain a large cadre of highly skilled, specialized workers. Instead, they rely on fewer, *less* skilled (and therefore cheaper) workers organized into "teams" who can perform all the assembly tasks required. The days of the high-priced, German-style industrial "craftsman" are gone, or going fast. Whole categories of skilled labor can be dispensed with in such a system. Indeed, that is one of its main selling points. Moreover, because the separate machine components are designed for easy production and assembly, a large corporation can further reduce costs by "outsourcing"—by contracting out as much production as possible to smaller, independent companies whose labor costs are lower than its own.[8] This means the parent company can get rid of many of its most costly workers (and their benefits), increase production by outsourcing to independent, competing (usually nonunion) firms, and increase profits while lowering costs all around.

In the service industries a similar development is also taking place. Here the role of information technology is paramount. The equivalent of simplified product design and assembly in this domain is the specialized software package. As Head puts it, "Just as Henry Ford once found a substitute for skilled craftsmen in rows of machines arranged along an assembly line, so the experts called reengineers have combined the skills of specialist clerks and middle managers into software packages that are attached to desktop computers."9 For example, underwriting insurance claims used to require several levels of specialists responsible for processing such claims from one department to the next. Now, using software that can perform most of those tasks with lightning speed and accuracy, a single employee of *lesser* skill than all of them can accomplish those same tasks at far less cost. Similarly for the processing of bank loans, credit card management, the filling of complex orders, plant management, auto sales, and wholesale purchases: Software can do the jobs of many specialists. Since 80 percent of Americans now work in service industries—banks, insurance companies, retail and wholesale outlets, hotels, and restaurants—the effects of such obsolescence and loss of jobs can be devastating.10

Ironically then, as companies achieve higher levels of productivity by simplified design, reengineering, and downsizing (laying workers off, especially expensive ones), their need for large numbers of *skilled* workers declines. This is mainly a broad trend in the manufacturing sector but also painfully affecting the service sector, especially middle management. Blue- and white-collar workers are now equally vulnerable not only to the effects of economic recession but to the effects of the new corporate success.

So, knowing who the losers are in the new, ruthless economy, who benefits from reengineering? Certainly the stockholders do as profits rise and costs decrease, but that's obvious. Who *within* the corporation benefits most?

CZARS AND TECHNOCRATS

Reengineering, Head observes, places great power in the hands of the creators of the new technologies of lean production and software packages that can transform a company's ways of doing business. He further observes:

> These high-level technocrats make up a large part of Felix Rohatyn's "technological aristocracy," and they are uniquely placed to influence the speed, direction, and scope of reengineering. But within the corporation they are also closely linked to another small group, the handful of top executives, led by . . . the reengineering "czar," who have the final say on investment decisions and who also have the power to hire and fire.[11]

I observed, firsthand, a situation very close to the one Head describes while consulting to Theo's insurance firm. I recall several confusing and, ultimately, devastating aspects of that situation. First, despite all the talk about reengineering among workers, hardly anybody really knew what it meant. Among middle managers, Theo was ahead of most because of his broad reading in business and economics. But not even he realized, second, that streamlining the routine activities of the business, that is, "becoming quick, flexible, and right" in their jargon, meant dispensing with their expert personnel!

The emphasis in the company's rhetoric was on "adaptability" not dispensability. The vague threat that those who could not adapt to organizational changes would not survive and that those who did would be a far more efficient "team" actually appealed to many—especially given the many bottlenecks and inefficiencies that blocked their daily efforts.

Third, nobody in middle management was privy to the top-level planning then in progress; but when several senior executives in the company abruptly resigned, others lower down in the hierarchy began to get uneasy. Will my division be dissolved? Will I be transferred elsewhere? How will I fit into the new organization? Still, few of those with expert skills and many years of service felt unduly threatened. After all, it was the company's right to demand of their best personnel that they adapt to new industry-wide demands and economic challenges. Another delusory smoke screen was the company's oft-repeated determination to "get back to the basic business of insurance"; in other words, to sell off its failing subsidiaries in real estate, banking, and the like. This too was welcomed as a sign of shrewd cutting of losses and renewed focus on what the company did best.

Fourth, most of the seasoned middle managers I talked with fully expected that a few senior heads would roll (as usually accompanies a reorganization) as well as those of the less-promising younger employees. "Tough on 'em, but they'll find their way elsewhere," one of the older managers said. Reengineering was, even at that late date, perceived as primarily *restructuring*, a "flattening" of management to put them all in closer touch with the customer, but not as downsizing in a way that would cost even the most experienced long-term employees their jobs. In other words, the company effectively disguised its real intentions by emphasizing employee efficiency and adaptability when, in fact, employee *dispensability* was its aim. Finally, when the ax did fall in 1990–91, it became apparent that the layoffs would not be in the hundreds but in the tens of thousands industry-wide.

Such naïveté on the part of experienced executives is no longer likely. It has happened too many times in too many businesses. The story has been told too many times in the media, and too many have personally lived through it. Had Theo been differently positioned within the company, he might well have been one of those guru-technocrats designing and implementing the new information technology and software, but he was too far away from the "Czar's" group to catch its eye. Anyway, reengineering on such a scale is usually carried out by the Czar's group in collaboration with independent consulting firms specializing in custom-tailored reengineering schemes.

Head mentions Michael Hammer and James Champy[12] as the leading proponents of reengineering. He also mentions their tendencies (1) to take credit for inventing something that, in one form or other, has been on the rise since the late 1960s and (2) to suggest that reengineering cannot be achieved successfully without outside consultants to wield the ax.[13] Head goes on to observe:

Hammer and Champy praise their clients—and, by implication, themselves—for carrying out the new and simpler divisions of the work force which reengineering makes possible. But the real stars of reengineering are the software and hardware packages that form the core of virtually every reengineering project. Without these packages there could be no consolidation of many tasks into a single task performed with a speed unimaginable in the pre-computer age, and no spectacular leaps of productivity.[14]

Software has no scruples. Hammer and Champy frankly admit that reengineering can create an atmosphere of distrust, anger, and panic, or in their words, "abject terror." They then go on to perpetuate the very same deception that Theo's company did. (Who knows, perhaps they were the consultants!) Acknowledging the distress and resistance of those who are "going to have to change what they do," Hammer and Champy suggest that "making it clear that termination is the consequence of their [employees'] behaviour is a very valid technique."[15] But that isn't the point really. Or rather, it's a callous misrepresentation of the real issue: job loss and personnel obsolescence, not mere change. It's too late to change if you've been declared redundant.

None of the middle managers I met at Theo's firm were computer-phobes, nor were any of the support staff. On the contrary, most were highly "computer literate." Nor were any of them so resistant to change in an industry subject to frequent corporate reshufflings as to risk their jobs. They had been through all that before, some many times. No, what they feared, or eventually woke up to, was loss of their jobs *whatever* their behavior.

Moreover, in the atmosphere of centralized, secretive power, there was no other power center (no union, no laws) to which to appeal or to represent their interests. "Nowhere," says Head, "are Hammer and Champy prepared to admit that employees have interests which ought to be the subject of negotiation and compromise."[16] Whatever its efficiencies, and they are conspicuous, reengineering has yet to acquire a human face. So far, it blames its victims for being unadaptable when, in fact, it renders them dispensable. The human costs just don't seem to matter.

THE BORDERLESS WORLD

Reengineering and its corollaries, lean production and downsizing, may be viewed as manifestations of even larger global economic trends likely to persist well into the twenty-first century. Paul Kennedy's *Preparing for the Twenty-first Century*[17] is, for my money, the best single volume on such trends and their probable effects on national economies over the next twenty-five years or so—the better part of your working life. As with the Simon Head piece, I will selectively abstract and modify some of Kennedy's observations as they pertain to the concerns of graduates in the hope of encouraging you further toward some survival reading.

The chief phenomenon influencing the shape and direction of corporate reengineering schemes is the rise of the new multinational companies and the kind of global competition they engender that pits workers from one part of the world against those in another. *Supranational* might be a better word to describe those companies, for they are increasingly detached from the culture, values, and local interests of their countries of origin. While originating, say, in Japan (Toyota, Sony), America (Union Carbide, Eli Lilly), or Germany (Siemens, Mercedes), they now operate globally with the world as their marketplace. Their primary sense of "place" is any place where production costs are relatively cheap and there is a market for their goods and services. For example, Kennedy quotes one senior American executive as saying, "The United States does not have an automatic call on our resources. There is no mind-set that puts the country first."[18] But there *is* a mind-set that puts the company first. This is crucial to understanding how and why the multinationals operate as they do.

Companies with *international* interests have been around for some time, assisted in their operations early on by the invention of the telegraph. In 1900 the House of Rothschild Bank had branches in Frankfurt, Paris, Vienna, and London; and Lloyds of London continued to compensate German shipping losses even after the outbreak of the 1914–18 war. Much later, Ford went international when it began to manufacture cars and trucks in Europe.[19] Coca-Cola and Bayer Aspirin also come to mind as omnipresent products the world over, not to mention Texaco (United States), Phillips Petroleum (United Kingdom), Noranda Mines (Canada), and the many oil and mining companies whose explorations have long spanned the globe.

I would describe these companies as more international than multinational or supranational, because up to the late 1960s they retained strong national identities and economic ties to their "home" offices. The United Fruit Company, for example, operated mainly out of Central and Latin America, but it was a decidedly American (even New England–style) company.

"But today's globalization," says Kennedy, "is distinguished from those earlier examples by the sheer quantity and extent of the multinational firms in our expanded and integrated economy."[20] Reduced national protectionism and liberalized exchange controls without the constraints imposed by central banks have combined to increase liquidity for world trade and stimulate the flow of transnational capital and foreign investments. While these developments helped to expand world commerce, they also had another effect: the separation of money markets from trade in manufactured products and services. "More and more, foreign-currency transactions took place not because a company was paying for foreign goods or investing in foreign assembly, but because investors were speculating in a particular currency or other financial instruments."[21]

Global capital flow began to take on a life of its own, apart from international trade and plant investments, with two further developments: "the deregulation of world money markets, and the revolution in global communications as a result of new technologies [computers, software, faxes, satellites, and the like]."[22] So far has this trend in currency flow gone that by the late 1980s more than 90 percent of the world's foreign exchange trade was unrelated to trade in manufactured goods or capital investment."[23]

This is the system within which today's multinational operates: producing and selling its products in all major economic regions, aiming not only to benefit from the scale of its business but also to protect itself from currency fluctuations, variable economic growth, and political interferences. As Kennedy puts it, "A recession in Europe will be of less concern to a firm which also operates in booming East Asian markets than to one exclusively dependent upon European sales."[24] This is also the "borderless world" in which the multinationals would ideally prefer that national governments and their agencies become invisible while those companies pursue "the new logic of the global marketplace."[25]

The optimists—mostly international bankers and consultants—point to the advantages to the consumer of the availability of a wider range of cheaper products; to companies, of vastly expanded markets; and to regions and nations, of attracting manufacturing and investments, provided, of course, they lower taxes and wage barriers, maintain a highly competent workforce, and open their cultures to the influx of information and influences from without. If they do, then the new global logic promises unbridled wealth, opportunity, and growth.

Pessimists, on the other hand, point to the corrosive effects on domestic markets, workers, and communities when a multinational decides to move its manufacturing and assembly elsewhere or to downsize radically, using the new technology, in order to remain competitive with other multinationals. In addition (as with the Thatcher-Major governments in Great Britain), economic nationalists fear that the international diffusion of manufacturing and finance erodes a nation's ability to control its own affairs.[26] It's not my purpose, nor Kennedy's, to take sides in this debate. But Kennedy does make one telling, cautionary point about the Pollyannaish "logic" of leaving everything to the controls of the free market:

> Indeed, the real "logic" of the borderless world is nobody is in control—except, perhaps, the managers of multinational corporations, whose responsibility is to their shareholders, who, one might argue, have become the new sovereigns, investing in whatever company gives the highest returns.[27]

Certain professions also are now internationalized, or becoming increasingly so, as the demand for their "added-value" services to multinationals increases. Kennedy mentions lawyers, biotechnology engineers, economic editors, software designers, and strategic planners, all of whom can operate from anywhere (using computers, faxes, and modems) to anywhere. In effect, "these creators and conveyors of high-added-value information are no longer linked to a regional or even a national economy."[28]

Many large companies with traditional links to communities, regions, and nations continue to exist, providing jobs for blue- and white-collar workers and prosperity to their communities; but they are under ever-growing pressure from international competition to reengineer and downsize, thus weakening those attachments to town and country. Hartford, Connecticut, for example, will remain an insurance center in the United States, but as friend Theo and his colleagues discovered, that onetime bastion of corporate stability is unlikely, at least for the foreseeable future, to provide the kind of job security for insurance workers that it once did.

If the foregoing fairly represents the broad economic forces at work in the world today and for some years down the line, what are the prospects for new college graduates?

HIGH SCHOOL JOBS FOR COLLEGE GRADUATES?

Stories abound of Ph.D.s driving taxis, of former senior executives personally downsized to menial labor, of highly skilled, aeronautical machinists turned auto mechanics, of lawyers working as bartenders. But what about recent college graduates? Their situation is not the same as older graduates or laid-off professionals and blue-collar workers. If you are one or about to graduate and look for work, the following may help to clarify your prospects and what you are up against.

In 1992 economist Daniel Hecker estimated that in 1990, 20 percent of all workers with college degrees were either unemployed or employed in jobs requiring only high school skills—in other words, McDonald's-level jobs. This percentage was up from a mere 11 percent in 1970.[29] The message was clear: We are turning out college graduates faster than we are creating jobs for them.

Coming in the midst of the early 1990s recession, Hecker's warning was quickly picked up in the popular press. *Newsweek's* Robert Samuelson, for example, wrote:

> [Hecker] convincingly demolishes the notion that there's a scarcity of college graduates and that sending more Americans to college will automatically create a more productive economy. . . . [If] more people had gone to college in the 1980s they would have competed mostly for lower-wage jobs that usually don't require a degree.[30]

Even were it so simple as that, many heretofore low-wage, low-skill jobs now require higher levels of skills, or at least higher skill levels than are readily available, to perform them. For example, Paul Kennedy writes:

> According to the Hudson Institute survey *Workforce 2000*, by the end of this century as many as 52 percent of *new* jobs may require at least some college education. . . . On the other hand, American industry has found it difficult to recruit workers to fill jobs not requiring a college education. The chairman of Xerox Corporation has declared that the skill levels of American society have "the makings of a natural disaster," while New York Telephone reports that it had to test a staggering 57,000 applicants to find 2,100 people to fill entry-level jobs.[31]

The problem of matching skills to jobs as thus stated admits of two interpretations: Either the skill levels to perform entry-level or "high school" jobs is rising (after all, even cash registers and telephone exchanges are computerized these days), or fewer applicants for such jobs possess the necessary skills, whatever they may be, to perform them. Probably both are true. Either way, that is no case *against* getting a college education. At the very least, while a college education is no guarantee of "appropriate" employment, it remains a strong asset for getting *any* job.

For example, Tyler, Murname, and Levey respond to Hecker's (or Hecker's readers') assumption that "a high school job is one which pays a high school wage even to a college graduate."

> College graduates in high school jobs will probably have lower earnings than other college graduates, but they may still earn more than high school graduates in similar jobs. Anecdotal evidence suggests that skill requirements have been rising within some occupational titles. If that has happened, it is possible that certain high school jobs now require college graduates and employers are willing to pay for them.[32]

In fact, the authors go on to demonstrate statistically not only the oft-cited earnings gap between B.A.s and high school graduates but "a growing differentiation between BAs and high school graduates *within high school jobs* which suggests that a BA has growing value even among those graduates who are doing most poorly."[33]

Without minimizing the difficulties of getting started in an atmosphere of white-collar reengineering and downsizing, the authors also present evidence to show that young B.A.s make substantial earnings gains throughout their twenties and on into their thirties. As mentioned earlier, young graduates often take two or three years to find themselves as well as a proper job. So "we should not let the anecdotes obscure the fact that newly minted B.A.s working in 'latte bars (or their equivalent) is nothing new, and that working in a 'latte bar at age 22 does not mean working in a 'latte bar at age 30."[34]

The morals to be drawn from these studies are sobering but not altogether negative. First, the value of a college education for future earning power (setting aside its personal value) is a demonstrated fact. Second, the younger college graduate stands a better chance of finding *some* employment and, eventually, desirable employment than the average high school graduate. Third, even college graduates working in high school jobs make higher wages than high school graduates in those same jobs.

And fourth, in the new, ruthless economy, the *younger* graduate is often far more employable than older, even highly qualified, experienced workers who have lost their jobs. That's not the most optimistic picture, but it's at least a hopeful one, especially if you are young, especially if you have been worrying about what your degree is worth, and especially if you have been feeling intimidated by the older, more experienced competition.

WHAT CAN I EXPECT? WHAT CAN I DO?

Whatever your level of college or professional education, you can expect to change jobs several times over your career. Despite the political hoopla in recent years over job training programs and their potential to solve the problems of unemployment and static or falling real wages, they are at best a stopgap measure. Many may no doubt profit from them in the way of training or retraining in marketable skills. "But it is an illusion," Head says, "to believe that such job programmes can by themselves recreate in significant numbers the secure, well-paid, and relatively high-skilled jobs that members of the middle class have traditionally held."[35] Indeed, Head reminds us, the higher rates of productivity, investments in information technology, creation of 8 million new jobs, and rising corporate profits have all been achieved without notable improvements in vocational education.[36]

That does not amount to an argument against preparing yourself as best you can for employment in a particular field or discipline; but it is an argument *for* being adaptable and staying that way. You may also want to ponder the fact that as the tide of domestic manufacturing recedes, the service industries are growing in relative importance. As mentioned, 80 percent of American workers are now employed in predominantly service jobs. They include, to mention only a handful, health and caring, teaching and retraining, airlines and travel, consultancies of every stripe, hotels and restaurants, the media, sports and fitness, construction, groundskeeping and snow removal, and every variety of wholesale and retail sales. As well, thanks to the new information technology, more people will be working out of their homes on desktop computers, using modems. For example, many publishing editors and literary agents already work that way, as do some software developers, graphic designers, and tax consultants.

In addition to your educational qualifications, there are several practical steps you can take to increase your adaptability. I base these suggestions on an informal survey of the experiences of recent job applicants with qualifications ranging from B.A.s to Ph.D.s seeking jobs in corporations, as consultants, as support staff, in service industries, and in academia.

If you hark back to the "Employers' Wish List" mentioned in Chapter One,[37] you will recall that literacy and numeracy are high on the list. Every applicant I spoke to emphasized the importance attached to the abilities to read carefully (often technical material), to write clearly and cogently, and to comprehend quantitative data (as in reading or producing spreadsheets). In some cases, higher mathematical skills were required, depending on the nature of the job. In every case, the stress given to "communication skills" demonstrated the importance employers place on them as *prerequisites* of employment. But that demand goes beyond basic literacy and numeracy. Most employers are seeking *high levels* of communication and quantitative skills in a variety of ways.

Trivial as it may sound, "a good telephone personality" was frequently mentioned. If you think about it, having a pleasant telephone manner can be essential, especially when dealing with the public or where the first customer contact with the business is over the telephone. Also, in these days of "teleconferencing," a forceful, yet pleasant telephone manner can make all the difference in whether a sale or a decision is made.

"People skills" were also mentioned often—the ability to work with others and to offer support and criticism with a minimum of abrasion. Sensitivity to the feelings of others, respect for their views, and the ability to keep even difficult disagreements on a "professional" plane are highly prized qualities. Most corporate thinking and problem solving, after all, are conducted in groups, not in isolation.[38] Discussion, which is to say, your ability to converse rationally, in depth, is a large part of what business calls people skills—not just being "nice." It behooves you, therefore, to develop your discussion and interpersonal skills in school, across a range of subjects and topics before you look for employment.

No less important, and tangential to discussion skills, is the ability to make a public presentation. More people fear public speaking than fear death. The stage fright that many people experience when asked to speak in public can be debilitating in the extreme; but there are proven ways of combating it.[39] If you have not already honed your public speaking skills in the course of your academic work, I strongly suggest that you take a short course in public speaking. Also, keep in mind the different circumstances in which you might be called upon to speak. Formal meetings, collegial discussions, technical presentations, informal presentations or lectures to the public, all place quite different demands on the speaker. The ability to speak clearly, calmly, to field questions and criticism without defensiveness, is a tremendous asset in the workplace.

Employers were also concerned with "character," such matters as dependability, punctuality, initiative, honesty, comportment, and ambition. While you have no direct control over how a prospective employer "reads" your character, your willingness to learn, to present yourself calmly and directly, to articulate your interest in the company, to ask intelligent questions, and to *listen* carefully will all go a long way toward leaving a favorable impression.

Listening is an especially important ability to cultivate, because when you speak, it's vital that you demonstrate that you have made an effort to understand what others have been saying, even if you disagree, indeed, especially if you disagree. The key to listening well is to listen not only for the content of what is said but also for the tone in which it is said and for the emotional effect it has.[40] Never underestimate or ignore the affect that surrounds what is said and how it is said. A calm demeanor of receptivity can be a powerful demonstration of your maturity and judgment. Employers are looking for that even if they do not say so in so many words.

Computer skills were less emphasized, not because they were not required but because they were *assumed*. The particular level of computer facility came up fairly often, however, depending on the demands of the job. They ranged from simple word processing to advanced financial, mathematical, and graphical skills. The plain fact of the matter is that familiarity with computers is taken to be a given among younger, college-educated employees. Most employers assume that you couldn't get through a good college program without them. In the words of Willy Loman in Arthur Miller's *Death of a Salesman*, "It comes with the territory."

Languages? It depends. In the new global economy and multinationals, languages can be a great asset. One woman I interviewed, a Ph.D. in financial planning, landed a splendid job with an international development banking concern doing business in the Caribbean and Latin America because, in addition to her obvious professional credentials, she also spoke fluent French, Spanish, English, and some Portuguese. She won out over dozens of other applicants in the interview when she demonstrated her ability to function in three of those languages with ease and tentatively in the fourth. She was also smart in aiming at a position that required precisely that combination of linguistic and professional expertise. A second or third language is a *credential* if you can connect it to your professional ambitions. However, nothing less than thorough fluency is likely to suffice in today's international market. Otherwise, forget it.

Critical thinking skills. An elusive notion but one that employers routinely stress in vague references to "problem solving" and "creativity." The idea here is to figure out what they are *really* after. The ability to conceptualize and analyze, to think independently and creatively, can, and often does, exist quite independently of a pleasing social manner. But unless you are fortunate enough to work alone—like a painter or writer—you will have to demonstrate those abilities in a social context. It's not just a matter of how well you think but of how convincingly you can present your ideas, sometimes in the face of opposition, that will determine how far your ideas will carry. Which brings us full circle, back to the stress that employers give to communication skills in all their variety. Employers are looking for personnel who can adapt and function effectively in tough, challenging circumstances that demand clear thinking, writing, and speaking. Play to that triune fact, and you just might get the job.

SUMMARY

This chapter began with an overview of the historical roots and emerging shape of the "new, ruthless economy," as it has come to be called, primarily because of its industrial reengineering schemes and downsizing that have put millions of blue- and white-collar workers out of work domestically and abroad. The combination of lean (simplified) production in manufacturing and powerful, fast software packages in the service industries has allowed companies to reduce costs by cutting their cadres of highly skilled workers, replacing them with fewer, less specialized workers, and outsourcing production to smaller, competing firms.

Reengineering has transferred power away from the unions and middle management to the hands of a few corporate "Czars" and their technological consultants who control both investments and hiring. Both Simon Head and I noted the tendency of reengineering schemes to ignore the human costs in their zeal to increase production and profits and to reduce costs. If software has no scruples, it seems that, so far, the reengineers don't either.

I went on to survey, with the help of Paul Kennedy, some of the broader causes of these developments in the rise of the new multinational corporations—or "supranationals," as I called them—which orchestrate production and wages on a global scale with little regard for local conditions except as they affect efficiency and maximum regard for increased production and shareholders' investments. Operating in a borderless world, they follow a global logic that promises unlimited wealth and access to consumer goods even as it deprives millions of a livelihood. Simultaneously creating thousands of new jobs in the added-value information technologies, their activities also result in a markedly uneven distribution of wealth and tend, in the opinion of some, to erode local, regional, and even national control. Others of a more optimistic view see the rise of the multinationals as a harbinger of a new global economy in which there will be no losers if only the megacompanies are left alone to respond to free market forces. Time will tell.

I went on to consider what all this might mean for the young college graduate. While the picture is not altogether bright, it is clear that a college degree is still a valuable asset in the new workplace and that even for those getting a slow start in so-called high school jobs, their earnings are likely to be higher; and they stand a much better chance of eventually finding desirable employment than high school graduates. Moreover, the younger graduate is far more employable than older, more educated and experienced workers who have been laid off—an advantage to at least one cohort of the ruthless economy.

Finally, I suggested some personal strategies of practical adaptability based on interviews with recent graduate applicants for a range of professional jobs. Beyond the technical proficiencies required (often high levels of literacy and numeracy), employers tended to emphasize certain personal qualities such as communications skills in many forms, from telephone personality to the ability to give public presentations; matters of comportment and professional conduct—people skills—with heavy emphasis on persuasiveness; and finally, adaptability to changing, often stressful conditions.

NOTES

1. Simon Head, "The New, Ruthless Economy," *New York Review of Books* 43, no. 4 (29 February 1996): 47–52.

2. Ibid., p. 47, col. 3.

3. Quoted in *Maclean's* magazine, 11 March 1996, p. 14.

4. Quoted in Head, "The New, Ruthless Economy," p. 47, col. 4.

5. Quoted in ibid.

6. Ibid., p. 49, col. 1.

7. Ibid., p. 47, col. 4.

8. Ibid., p. 48, col. 2.

9. Ibid., p. 47, col. 4.

10. See the recent (March 1996) *New York Times* series "The Downsizing of America," especially the 5 March piece entitled "Big Holes Where Dignity Used to Be." Available on the Web at http://www.nytimes.com/downsize.

11. Head, "The New, Ruthless Economy," p. 50, col. 1.

12. See Michael Hammer and James Champy, *Reengineering the Corporation: A Manifesto for Business Revolution* (New York: Harper Business, 1993); and Michael Hammer and Steven A. Stanton, *The Reengineering Revolution: A Handbook* (New York: Harper Business, 1995).

13. Head, "The New, Ruthless Economy," p. 49, col. 1.

14. Ibid., pp. 49–50, cols. 3 and 1.

15. Quoted in ibid., p. 50, col. 2.

16. Ibid.

17. Paul Kennedy, *Preparing for the Twenty-first Century* (New York: Random House, 1993).

18. Ibid., p. 58.

19. Ibid., p. 50.

20. Ibid.

21. Ibid.

22. Ibid.

23. Ibid., p. 51.

24. Ibid.

25. Ibid., p. 55.

26. Ibid., pp. 52–53.

27. Ibid., p. 55.

28. Ibid., p. 59.

29. Daniel E. Hecker, "Reconciling Conflicting Data on Jobs for College Graduates," *Monthly Labor Review* (July 1992): 3–12.

30. Robert J. Samuelson, "The Value of College," *Newsweek*, 31 August 1992, p. 75. Quoted along with other press versions of Hecker's findings in John Tyler, Richard J. Murname, and Frank Levey, "Are Lots of College Graduates Taking High School Jobs? A Reconsideration of the Evidence," Working Paper No. 5127 (Washington, D.C.: National Bureau of Economic Research, May 1995), p. 2.

31. Kennedy, *Preparing for the Twenty-first Century*, pp. 314–15.

32. Tyler, Murname, and Levey, "Are Lots of College Graduates," p. 4.

33. Ibid., p. 13; italics theirs.

34. Ibid., p. 16.

35. Head, "The New, Ruthless Economy," p. 51, col. 1.

36. Ibid.

37. See Chapter 1.

38. See V. A. Howard and J. H. Barton, *Thinking Together: Making Meetings Work* (New York: William Morrow, 1992), chap. 1, "On the Nature of Rational Discussion."

39. See ibid., chap. 2, "Overcoming Stage Fright."

40. See ibid., "Listening and Responding," pp. 148–54.

CHAPTER SIX
STARTING OVER

FRESH AND STALE STARTS

Ending this book with a chapter on starting over when you are barely starting out may seem like crossing purely imaginary bridges long before you come to them—until you consider the fact that crossing the school/work divide is itself a *kind* of starting over. Leaving school at any level for the workplace can be a daunting experience of starting over for anyone, even for those moving smoothly from specialized studies, say, in law or business, to employment in a corresponding field. Short of that, a change of major or concentration in school also constitutes at the very least a change of mind or heart that could be described as starting over, a refocusing of one's interests.

Indeed, liberal, as contrasted with vocational, education is an exercise in experimentation, in repeatedly starting over for the sake of discovery and exposure to a variety of fields and perspectives. That's its value as contributing to self-growth and experimentation in a "protected" environment that encourages risk taking without dire consequences. Yet the exploratory whole is in partial preparation for future, real-life contingencies. The more you know, the more you *can* know and learn. That's the

real payoff and value of a liberal education. It is the most
practical base from which to begin.

Seen in this light, nearly any subject you take up may acquire
borrowed interest. The objective, ultimately, is not merely to
master the intricacies of econometrics, philosophical analysis,
or mineralogy but to find yourself, what you want, what you do
best, what prospects you may have as an artist, scholar, engineer, or businessperson.

A fresh start. A new enterprise. Nothing could be more exhila-
rating or stimulating. Rushing down new corridors of thought
and action like a child at a toy fair. You can see it on the faces of
your fellow students at the beginning (if not always at the
middle or end!) of term. That's the positive, somewhat romantic
side of starting over. Don't knock it. Romance is a great adven-
ture in any domain, not just in love affairs. It fuels our interest
and devotion and can lead to great things: to accomplishment,
to a vocation, to undreamed-of fulfillment.

Other starts begin on a rather stale note: an examination in
calculus failed (so much for engineering); your piano teacher
takes you aside and tells you that a concert career is not for you;
the area in which you are working is suddenly eliminated from
your company. A road taken ends in tangled underbrush. So you
have to start over. That is what this last chapter is about:
starting over, by chance, by choice, or by necessity—whether in
a burst of fresh enthusiasm or a bust of stale disappointment.

OOPS! WHAT NOW?

"Ah, Jane, I called you in to have a little chat about your work
for us in the AI Division."

"Oh, fine, Bill, we have some really wonderful new projects
going on predicting short-term, irrational behavior based on
Herrnstein's model of—"

"No, Jane, what I mean is, well, you must be aware of the
cutbacks we've been experiencing in basic research—in fact, all
around the company. I'm afraid the front office has decided to
further reduce personnel in the AI Division. We're due to lose
ten positions there, and while your work for us has been excellent, you've been with us for only eighteen months, I see. Well,

that's six months short of our first rung of employee security. I mean, a number of people higher up the ladder have already received their notices this morning. Really, Jane, it's out of my hands."

Oops! That's how quickly and unexpectedly it can happen. Oh, there may have been rumors of future layoffs and lots of rumblings about restructuring, downsizing, and leveling of management, but Jane was doing really important work for the company. Her quarterly ratings were top-notch, and she was scheduled for promotion in six months, not a pink slip. Her stomach turns over; she fights back the tears but manages to hold form. She leaves the vice-president's office hardly hearing the assurances of "every assistance," "fine references," "a great future, Jane." Yeh, but not at Consolidated Industries. And all that *work* . . .

That's one way of starting over: getting fired or laid off. After she recovers from the initial shock, Jane will likely accept the company's offer of excellent references and job search assistance (usually through the mediation of an independently contracted placement firm) and look for similar work at another company in, say, robotics or computer software. Jane is young—in her late twenties, highly skilled, proven on the job, and perhaps most important, *marketable*. Unlike our old pal Theo, she is qualified without being overqualified for an entry-level position. She comes cheaper and lower than he can ever hope to be, even if he were willing. Although perhaps less versatile at her work than he might be, given his immense technical range, she stands a much better chance of reemployment in the area of her expertise than he does. We covered some of this ground in the previous chapter. The moral is clear: Don't expect justice in the "ruthless economy"; learn to live with it.[1]

There are other stories of starting over that begin even earlier in life. Jennifer Capriati turned tennis pro at age thirteen, winning the Puerto Rican Open in 1990. By 1991, at fifteen, she was the twenty-sixth wealthiest athlete in the world. In 1992 she won a gold medal at the Olympic Games in Barcelona. After several more major tournament wins, she lost to Monica Seles in the first round of the U.S. Open in August of 1993. Despondent, she dropped out of professional tennis, and in late 1993 and the Spring of 1994, she was brought up on charges of shoplifting and possession of marijuana in Florida.[2] Oops!

Commenting on the aftermath of her loss to Seles at the U.S. Open, she said:

> I started out O.K., but at the end of the match I couldn't wait to get off the court. Totally, mentally, I just lost it . . . and obviously it goes deeper than that one match. I really was not happy with myself, my tennis, my life, my parents, my coaches, my friends. . . . I spent a week in bed in darkness after that, just hating everything. When I looked in my mirror, I actually saw this distorted image: I was so ugly and so fat, I just wanted to kill myself, really.[3]

After court-approved rehabilitation, Capriati staged a comeback at the ripe old age of eighteen! Her renewed interest in tennis, however, rested on a reconsideration of what tennis meant to her. "It's just a game to me now," she said, one for which she had conspicuous talent she didn't want to waste. "I don't care about being No. 1, but I'm ready and willing to give battle, and that's what sports is all about. . . . Just give me a racquet. There's no ending to my story yet."[4] But it will be a different story. Still in her early twenties, Jennifer Capriati recently retired from professional tennis.

Here you see a dramatic reconstruction of the Self on task in which Jennifer's self-identity is no longer completely wrapped up in tennis or being the absolute best at it—a valuable lesson to learn at so young an age. Having achieved a measure of psychic distance from her all-consuming passion, she may retain some connection with tennis; or if she does not, it will not destroy her. Jane, the AI whiz, is starting over after losing her job. Jennifer is starting over after burning out. Both had to *let go* of something involuntarily—a job, a conception of the self—in order to start over again. There are less dramatic cases of letting go, rather more voluntary or predictable in nature, that also deserve notice as life patterns even as you are starting out to work.

LETTING GO: I SHALL, I MUST

The most obvious case is retirement. While retirement may appear an altogether premature topic for graduates on the brink of work to bother with, consider this an exercise in clarifying present and short-term uncertainties in terms of a future certainty. Most professions have a mandatory retirement age, usually around age sixty-five. Early retirement, as early as fifty or fifty-five, is an increasing trend in some industries under the economic or technological pressures of rapid change, as we have seen. What then?

I'm not asking you to try to answer that remote question now, only to consider that it *will* happen. Moreover, your choice of profession now greatly influences what your options will be then. I'm told by people in advertising, for example, that anyone entering that field had better be prepared for the fact that it is a young person's game, that you will have risen as far as you ever shall by your midforties. After that, it's hanging on at best unless you are at the top. With few exceptions (and they are the ones we tend to focus on), rock musicians, athletes, models, actors, and the like, have notoriously short careers and time in which to "make it." Most are washed up by their mid- to late thirties. Certain professions seem tailored to fit F. Scott Fitzgerald's dictum, "There are no second acts in American lives."5

Fitzgerald notwithstanding, there *are* second, even third, acts in many people's lives, even if not the ones they expected or hoped for. In our professional as in our personal lives, the second or third time around may be even better. Consider the case of Dan L., a former colleague of mine at a Canadian university. When I met him, Dan was an ex-football pro, high school teacher of art, and coach who had been appointed Professor of Art Education at my university. Then in his fifties, Dan did not fit the stereotype of the university professor. He had no Ph.D., no publications of note, and he was something of an inveterate "jock." Working out with him almost daily, I listened to his litany of complaints: academic snobbery, professors of curriculum who knew nothing about the realities of high school teaching, a skeptical dean who blocked his every move and advancement, a university establishment that took little notice of his abilities as a painter and teacher of teachers.

Years later after I had left, Dan retired from the university frustrated and on the brink of a nervous breakdown. He and his wife took off on an extended tour of the American Southwest. His second act seemed to have come to a sad end.

But Dan *was* a talented portrait and landscape painter. Gradually, his paintings of the Southwest (in Canadian "Group of Seven" style) caught the eye of gallery owners across America and Canada. His wide network of former athletes and coaches tapped him to paint their portraits. He is now, at age seventy-seven, much in demand as a portrait painter of famous athletes, coaches, club owners, and of all things, academic deans and university presidents! His third act, an extension of his first, turned out better than the previous two.

Yet others start over in more deliberate, calculated fashion. Sam W. was a New York City policeman pounding a beat in his midforties when he decided to take early retirement and go back to graduate school. Admitted to graduate studies in education, he took a master's and doctoral degrees in educational psychology. For several years thereafter, he was a popular professor of psychology and education at a large urban university.

A colleague of mine, who was his former thesis advisor, discovered that after retirement from teaching Sam went back to school again, this time to study law. Practicing pro bono law in the small Cape Cod community to which he and his wife had moved, he was cited for his efforts on behalf of those unable to afford legal representation. Drawn thereby into local politics, he was elected alderman of the town. An altruistic thread unified Sam's police, educational, legal, and political work: a determination to see to it that people got the help they needed. Like Jennifer Capriati, though at the opposite end of the life scale and with no competitive self-advantage in mind, Sam was equally determined not to waste his talents.

Running through these otherwise quite different examples of starting over is the ability to let go of one thing or ambition while consolidating past gains and experience (including one's mistakes) toward a new goal that fits a broadening moral vision. Unlike the highly successful but unfulfilled Peter J. of an earlier chapter, these people, even single-minded Jane, would have little trouble answering the questions, Why am I doing this?

What do I owe myself? For each of them, the significance of those two questions did (or will) alter in significance throughout the life cycle. That is perhaps the main point for anyone starting out to realize; namely, that sometime, somehow, somewhere, you will have to start over.

PROFESSIONS THAT DO / PROFESSIONS THAT DON'T

Some professions seem to lend themselves to natural transitions better than others. Erik Erikson, the distinguished psychoanalyst and chronicler of the life cycle,[6] returned to part-time work in a mental hospital after a long career of teaching, research, and writing to serve in an advisory capacity to his younger colleagues, many of whom he had trained. Phyllis Curtin, the Metropolitan Opera soprano mentioned earlier,[7] went on to a second career in teaching and arts administration at Boston University. Indeed, she was one of the longest-serving deans in that institution's history. And, of course, there are many instances of athletes turned coaches, of public figures turned writers, of housewives turned real estate dealers (who better knows what couples are looking for?), of priests and nuns turned social workers and teachers. Calculated second, even third and fourth, acts do happen, can be made to happen.

But what about the insurance or advertising executive, the firefighter, the automobile salesperson, the engineer, or the corporate administrative assistant? It's not at all clear what second act, consistent with the first, could follow. There are exceptional individuals like William Warner who retired from the U.S. State Department to write a Pulitzer Prize–winning book,[8] but that was an outgrowth of a long-standing, independent interest. And not everyone has such a consuming passion for learning as Theo, the artistic talent of Dan L., or the altruistic bent of Sam W. What of the others? Must their expertise and hard-won experience go to waste?

We live in a culture that gives little consideration to that question beyond platitudes about the "golden years" and "well-earned rewards" of leisure in retirement—a time when many feel themselves dying on the vine, slipping into atrophy and decline. What can be done about it? What can *you* do about it?

What do you owe to yourself and to them in this regard? Anything?

I put the question bluntly to underscore three points: first, that it is in your interest to benefit from the seasoned experience and perspective of disinterested elders in your chosen field (by whom I mean those no longer in competition with you); second, so that you may be better prepared for inevitable changes to come; and third, so that what you learn in the course of your career may become available to the next generation. It's only common sense that this is the most cost-efficient way to proceed both in personal and professional terms. So, to repeat, what can you do?

If you are fortunate enough to have an older mentor, discuss his or her future plans as a tentative guide to your own. Not only will that give you some insight into life's stages, but it may also encourage your mentor to explore further options for service and self-development. People's motives and ambitions change with age, and the more you can learn about such changes early on, the better prepared you will be for them when they happen to you.

Second, you can take note of the many midlife career training programs that have sprung up in corporations and educational institutions. Once ensconced in a job, you can afford a moment from time to time to examine what your company or others like it are doing to assist personnel to make changes, alter their career directions, or upgrade their skills. Such programs, whether in-house or available from independent educational or professional organizations, are always worth a look-see if for no other reason than to keep your mind open to future options and opportunities. Consider this a plea for your support of a *policy* of renewal in the workplace, one that may well benefit you later on.

Whole professions, seemingly secure, may undergo drastic changes under adverse economic and political pressures. Today's high roller may be on his hands and knees tomorrow. Bill B., a friend of mine, president for several years of his own electronics engineering firm closely allied with the defense industry, found himself bereft of clients and low on capital when the federal government cut back on defense spending in 1992. Only months before his company collapsed, he was honored at a White House reception as one of the most successful black entrepreneurs in American business. Oops! What now?

Marshaling his resources, Bill quickly recouped, securing a senior position with a major consulting and research firm. A year later, after a company shake-up and downsizing, his division was dissolved and his position with it. Two tough blows within a year and a half. Wisely, Bill, who is nearing fifty, has decided to take a different tack. He is applying for a year's university fellowship for minority professionals with potential for educational administration and government service. He is a prime candidate, given his technical and administrative expertise, and I have no doubt that he will find his level among his peers in the program. A whole new network will come out of it, opening new doors of opportunity for a man of demonstrated ability. In the meantime, he suffers and wonders and worries. What will become of me? What shall I do? A shy man, quietly spoken and dignified, he *needs* the stimulus of an organized program to get the best out of him. It will; he will. So I say, knowing him well and wishing him the best. But he must live with the uncertainty.

This is the sort of thing you need to think about in quieter moments in your day-to-day activities. What will I do if . . . ? What kind of person am I? What is best for me? It can't hurt, and your farsightedness will pay off in terms of new opportunities and career options that might not have occurred to you earlier on. In that sense, experience is a good teacher—but only if it is active and reflective. Accordingly, I want to consider now what it means to learn from experience—or to get trapped by it. Our natural respect for experience tends to blind us to the fact that it is a double-edged sword cutting off options even as it opens new ones. In the poignant words of Robert Frost's "The Road Not Taken":

> Two roads diverged in a yellow wood,
> And sorry I could not travel both and be one
>   traveler,
> Long I stood and looked down one as far as I could
> To where it bent in the undergrowth;
> Then took the other as just as fair,

And having perhaps the better claim,
Because it was grassy and wanted wear;
Though as for that the passing there
Had worn them really about the same,
And both that morning equally lay
In leaves no step had trodden black.
Oh, I kept the first for another day!
Yet knowing how way leads on to way,
I doubted if I should ever come back.
I shall be telling this with a sigh
Somewhere ages and ages hence:
Two roads diverged in a wood,
And I—I took the one less traveled by
And that has made all the difference.[9]

When it comes to a major decision in life, a choice of one thing is usually at the expense of another. The decision to pursue medical studies probably means dropping, at least deferring, that secondary dream of being a professional writer or jazz saxophonist. Maybe not, as an avocation or sideline; but not likely as a full-time occupation. Oh, you may keep the latter for another day—make a complete switchover. It's been done. Yet, knowing how way leads on to way . . .

LEARNING FROM EXPERIENCE

Early on, I noted that the old saw about experience being the best teacher can be mightily misleading if left at that.[10] To be significant, experience requires being interpreted, which is to say, understood and evaluated. *An* experience, one having significance, John Dewey tells us, "has a unity that gives it its name, *that* meal, that storm, that rupture of friendship. The existence of this unity is constituted by a single *quality* that pervades the entire experience in spite of the variation of its constituent parts."[11] In other words, a significant experience is one that stands out against the backdrop of humdrum indifference or rigid routine (habit) as having both identity and feeling tone, what Dewey calls the "aesthetic stamp" upon notable lived experiences.[12]

Whether experiences turn out after the fact to have been predominantly intellectual, practical, or emotional (as identified), "in their actual occurrence they were emotional as well" (as felt).[13] You may also recall that for Dewey significant experience can be canceled out by either an "excess of receptivity" (passivity) or an "excess of doing" (frenetic activity).[14] Underdoing or overdoing may equally blind us to the significance of events.

In sum, having *gone through* something, even surviving some catastrophe, or having merely *done* something for a long time is insufficient by itself to teach us anything. We all know individuals who seem not to have learned much from their experiences in school, at work, or in life. The dull teacher lecturing tediously from old notes, the indifferent student, the chronic heart patient who refuses to change his smoking or dietary habits, the corporate executive buried in mindless routine, the war veteran who takes no interest in the historical events that framed the battles he survived—all seem unwittingly, if not willfully, to truncate the significance of their experiences.

Bare recognition and preestablished habit are enough to get through most situations without learning much from them. "Bare recognition," says Dewey, "is satisfied when a proper tag or label is attached, 'proper' signifying one that serves a purpose outside the act of recognition—as a salesman identifies wares by a sample."[15] Nothing stirs, nothing arouses. We simply take note of the thing in a receptive, largely passive way. An act of *perception*, on the other hand, is "emotionally pervaded throughout."[16] Perception requires energy and effort, a measure of activity that goes beyond mere recognition. In Dewey's words,

> Perception is an act of the going-out of energy in order to receive, not a withholding of energy. To steep ourselves in a subject-matter we have first to plunge into it. When we are only passive to a scene, it overwhelms us and, for lack of answering activity, we do not perceive that which bears us down. We must summon energy and pitch it at a responsive key in order to *take* in.[17]

Nothing is given in perception but that it must also be taken in order to amount to significant experience. "For to perceive, a beholder must *create* his own experience."[18] Now, Dewey ventured these remarks on experience and the distinction between recognition and perception as part of his demonstration that aesthetic perception is not "an affair for odd moments,"[19] something segregated from ordinary life and practical concerns. (Recall his discussion of the business interview from Chapter Two.)[20] Inasmuch as *all* significant experience in his view exhibits an aesthetic stamp, it is easy to see why he favors a continuum between art and life rather than a sharp separation. But my concern here is not with art as such, although I have had a good deal to say about its relevance to everyday life and work. Rather, my concern is with how we learn or fail to learn from experience, be it intellectual, aesthetic, practical, or emotional.

Consider again Dan L. He hit a stone wall of academic indifference, even snobbery, as regards his artistic, teaching, and sports experience. Ten years of that nearly broke his spirit. He *recognized* full well what he was up against, but he could do nothing about it. Once liberated from that situation, however, his artistic *perception* carried him to new heights of achievement and acclaim for his work. Ironically, as mentioned earlier, he is much in demand these days as a lecturer and studio artist at colleges and universities. In Dewey's words, he pitched his energies at a responsive key, refusing to be overwhelmed.

Or consider Bill B. Surveying his engineering, administrative, and business experience, he has decided to steep himself in a new subject matter, to plunge into it, in what might be described as a *lateral* career move—one that builds on that experience in a new direction. He recognizes that the old options are closed for political and economic reasons and perceives that he must strike out anew. That is what it means to learn from experience: an increase in strategic and moral vision based on what has gone before. Both men met adversity with an "answering activity."

In their several ways, Jane, Jennifer Capriati, Dan L., Sam W., and Bill B. are persons of developed or developing sensibilities. Their judgment, whatever the vicissitudes of their lives, is not submerged under a bureaucracy or reflex routine. They are not rooted in the done thing. Like friend Theo, they are not undone by having the rug pulled out from under them. They are trapped neither by their past accomplishments nor by the sudden loss of status or position.

Uncomfortable, even dire circumstances are manageable for such individuals precisely because they have invested themselves *in themselves* first and only then in this or that job or institution. It remains only to say that such individuals have a more superior capacity than many to adjust, to adapt, to renew themselves and take on new challenges.

As I write these lines, I cannot avoid mention of a whole people who seem stricken by paralysis, unable to adjust or to find an "answering activity." In 1993, the Newfoundland cod fishery was shut down by the Canadian government. Depleted cod stocks, the result of decades of overfishing and ecological damage, necessitated the decision. Hundreds of fishermen were suddenly deprived of a traditional livelihood that reaches back four centuries. With so much vested in one industry, the Newfoundland economy is in ruin. A once proud and independent people are humiliated, demoralized, with few prospects. (As of the summers of 1994 to 1997, the cod stocks were in even worse shape than predicted.)

Coming from a fishing family myself, I can sympathize with their plight. Condemned to the dole for as long as it lasts, one can only wonder, What will these people do? What will become of them? Many have left "The Rock" in search of work elsewhere, but lacking marketable skills, their prospects are not good. Then, I remember something my grandfather said to me long ago on Grand Manan, an island in the Bay of Fundy where we lived then: "Don't go on the boats, lad. The fisheries will be finished in twenty years. Find a land job. Get more education." Reluctantly, I took his advice. Admittedly, having a taste for music and books that many of my contemporaries lacked, the decision was perhaps inevitable. Still, it was a hard choice at the time, but deferring to his experience and strategic vision, I left that life behind. Otherwise, I might now be one of the permanently unemployed, possessed of obsolete sea skills, a mortgaged ship and home, a family to support, with nowhere to sail and no fish to catch. I am grateful to him for his foresight and tough counsel.

Looking back, I see that his experience had something to teach me, something that *at the time* I could not see clearly for myself. But I trusted him and listened with care. Having little experience of my own to draw on then, it was his forward vision that saved me from personal disaster down the line. That is why I think it is so important not to waste our elders' lessons of long years on task: simply to avoid personal disaster. Beyond that, we have much to learn for ourselves but only if we keep ourselves in a posture of "answering activity" to life's challenges.

FALSE STARTS

Despite my recommendation to sound the knowledge and experience of mentors and elders selectively, advice from such quarters is not always reliable or beneficial. Indeed, unless tempered with wisdom, it can be downright misleading, even destructive. It's a sensitive topic and one I've deliberately left until now. As mentioned, long experience and time on task can harden opinion as readily as it can, with answering activity, expand one's vision and deepen one's judgment. Parents, teachers, and mentors can be blindly insensitive, even ruthless, in the pursuit of their own ambitions through the agency of their children, students, or protégés.[21] Even with the best of intentions, one may be set off in the wrong direction. Accordingly, any chapter dealing with the prospect of starting over, voluntarily or not, including fresh and stale starts, cannot avoid the topic of false starts.

The logical key to understanding false starts is that not everything you can or feel obliged (or pressured) to do is necessarily what you may want or should do. As in track and field, a false start is a matter of "jumping the gun." For example, a lot of young people just out of college go into law, business, or medical school for economic or prudential reasons: because of financial security (often hastily presumed), because they cannot think of anything more creative to do, or because of parental pressure. The itchy-palmed, heedless, or coerced decision to enter upon a professional regimen—even where one is quite up to the demands—can easily lead to early burnout, frustration, and despair.

The conflict is as old as the ancient distinction between job and vocation mentioned in Chapter One.[22] A poignant example of the crisis engendered by a false start is to be found in the life and works of America's first major novelist, Charles Brockden Brown.[23] Between 1789 and 1800, up to his thirtieth year, Brown wrote five novels—*Wieland, Ormond, Arthur Mervyn, Edgar Huntly,* and *Memoirs of Stephen Calvert*—in all of which, according to Robert Ferguson, "he used his fiction as a fantasy world for projecting occupational difficulties":

> For Brown the moment of vocational choice always remained distinct and ominous. "It behooves us," he told the members of his early literary society, "to make preparations for that awful crisis in choosing our future parts." Later he added that "the first step . . . is frequently the point on which fate hangs suspended, and may elevate us to an eminent height of happiness, or sink us into the profoundest abyss of misery." These fears grew out of a particular crisis in 1793 when Brown rejected the law as his profession after six years in the Philadelphia law offices of Alexander Wilcocks. The decision led to permanent disapproval from family and friends, and it plunged Brown into a five-year period of aimless unhappiness, a personal abyss of misery central to the dark patterns of the later novels.[24]

Fleeing in 1793 to New York and the company of a handful of kindred literary spirits, he escaped conventional pressures, but only for a time (until 1800). In the meantime, Brown's merchant father and four working brothers in Philadelphia awaited the return of the "idle" fifth son to assume his dutiful place in the family business, constantly badgering him to do so forthwith. Postcolonial America's small circle of intelligentsia were contemptuous of Brown's "fickleness of purpose" and the "poor sophistry" by which he rejected the legal profession. As Ferguson remarks, "Fiction lacked respectability as a literary genre in

Federalist America, while law represented a major topic of general interest within the realm of letters. When William Wirt and countless others announced that 'the bar in America is the road to honour,' they meant that law provided the best intellectual challenge as well as the most convenient avenue to wealth and preferment."[25]

Unable to support himself, tormented by his being "a mere holder of the pen" who has "often resolved to cast it away, tired and ashamed of its incorrigible depravity,"[26] Brown returned to Philadelphia in late 1800 to take his assigned place in the family firm, never to write fiction again. Admittedly, Brown's predicament was partly self-induced and partly circumstantial. "While the novelist used law [in his fiction] to illustrate misgivings about the world, he continued to accept the social standards that made his own position such an uncomfortable one."[27] The respectable literary genres of eighteenth-century America were civic and philosophical, not fictional or poetic. Brown never managed to reconcile art and utility in a way that would diminish the conflict within himself or that between himself and the society in which he lived. "Accommodation—the desire to appear useful in an age of utility—required some kind of integration of the artist within society, and Brown clearly saw the problem in his fiction. Nevertheless, and despite many attempts, a life of frustration kept him from finding a meaningful imaginative solution."[28] Brown went against the grain, but the grain ran too deeply within his own soul.

Brown's story of a false start for which he could find no true solution, sad as it is (not to mention the loss to American literature), clearly illustrates the guilt and torment that often beset forced or faulty beginnings in professional life. But more subtle, less self-evident false starts can be equally insidious in their long-term effects. Self-deception and -delusion dog us all in one form or other through life, but none so much as those of exceptional ability combined with dutiful obeisance. I have in mind some students who, from an early age, and usually of high intelligence, demonstrate exceptional scholastic aptitude across a broad range of academic subjects. Having few weaknesses, relatively speaking, and experiencing mostly success, they are seldom driven to identify their true strengths or, you might say, their heart's desire. They differ from the ordinary by their exceptional scholastic and possibly other (athletic, social) abilities. But equally, they differ from extraordinary, creative individuals who often experience severe setbacks and are forced to find their bliss in being expert at the "done thing." They succeed by conforming. You might think of them as Brown's nemeses!

Howard Gardner has studied how truly exceptional people—great innovators in their respective fields like Freud, Virginia Woolf, Gandhi, Darwin—differ from ordinary mortals. Besides reflecting deeply on the events large and small of their lives (nothing too surprising in that), and exhibiting remarkable ability to recover from setbacks and failures (exceptional confidence and determination—important personality traits), "Extraordinary individuals are distinguished less by their impressive 'raw powers' than by their ability to identify their strengths and then to exploit them."[29] Now *there* is a useful insight into how the extraordinary departs from the ordinary. Many individuals, including those of conspicuous talent, never succeed in finding their strengths and are undone by their weaknesses. Brown got off to a false start, then discovered his bliss but could not sustain it. But there are other true stories of false starts with happier endings, or rather, happier prospects for new beginnings.

In the February 1992 issue of *Harvard Magazine*, there appears an article entitled "Free of the Law" by Glenn Kaye. In it, Kaye recounts the experiences of several recent and not-so-recent graduates of the Harvard Law School for whom the law turned out to be not for them. Similar pieces turn up from time to time in various alumni magazines and academic newsletters about disaffected individuals in medicine, business, or education, most of whom, as in Kaye's article, hardly knew what they were getting into despite their success in getting into it.[30] It is important to stress, however, that the individuals Kaye interviewed were not failures either as students or as lawyers. Far from it! Graduating at or near the top of their undergraduate classes, they are all graduates of one of the country's elite law schools and at the time of their crises were working, often outstandingly well, for distinguished law firms. Coincidentally, most of them resemble Brown in being about four to six years out in their careers before questioning their choice of law as a life's work. Kaye opens with the story of Nora (not her real name):

> Nora, a young lawyer seven years out of Harvard, works for one of the biggest, fanciest firms in New York. It's a "white shoe" establishment, where maps of colonial New England line the walls and identical bouquets of pink lilies decorate the receptionists' mahogany desks. The firm is an easy walk to the West Side sushi bars Nora likes to frequent. When she returns to her office after lunch, she is greeted by her collection of glittering lucite cubes, each encasing a miniature newspaper announcement of a big corporate deal she helped close.
>
> Nora's firm, with its clublike ambiance, may seem a paradise to some. But despite its lush furnishings — and the $165,000-a-year salary it pays her — Nora loathes the place. She'd be delighted, she confides, if she never saw another colonial map or another lucite "deal toy" again.
>
> Lately Nora, 32, has been plotting a different life. At night and on weekends, she is discreetly sending out resumés, hoping to convince a museum or concert hall to hire her as an administrator. The moment she finds such a job, she promises, "I'm out of here."[31]

Before examining Nora's own reasons for wanting to get out of a lucrative and successful law practice, it's enlightening to hear the views of Leona Vogt, a Cambridge-based career counselor, whom Kaye also interviewed, whose clientele is mainly lawyers seeking to make a change. "What sets them [lawyers] and her other high-achieving clients apart, she explains, is *their brilliance in fulfilling other people's expectations rather than their own.*"[32] The competitive focus of law school, as of the law itself, is "outward," she continues. "This means that even highly accomplished lawyers can be sorely lacking in self-knowledge. . . . They are not used to an inward focusing. . . . It is not an easy task for those who have always looked to others for approval. . . . I ask them, 'When you think of the joy that you've experienced in life, what comes to mind?' They don't even know what the word means. They say, 'What do you mean by *joy*? Do you mean success, achievement, satisfaction?' "[33]

There is the key to most false starts: an inability to distinguish what *you* want (what you owe yourself, to repeat an old theme) from what others expect of you. In the words of Harvard Law School's own career counselor Mark Byers, "They are so consistently rewarded for doing their best—and Harvard has been part of that reward—that they no longer recognize what they like doing. Or they are torn between what they like and what is purported to be the best."[34] Another factor is lack of forward planning, or more simply put, knowing what you are getting into.

Larry Richard, who runs a Philadelphia career-advisory service for lawyers, picks up on that theme. Since most any undergraduate major will suffice to get into law school (other graduate programs have more tightly prescribed preprofessional requirements), applying to law school is a "natural" for undergraduates who are not quite sure what they want to do. "Even when the decision to apply to law school is not made on the spur of the moment, Richard says, it is often grounded on shaky logic. 'The person who does not have a clear career goal as an undergrad, but does want to be a professional, often employs a process-of-elimination methodology: I don't like the sight of blood, so forget about medicine; I'm not good at numbers, so I'll rule out accounting; I don't have a visual sense, so I'll rule out architecture,' he says."[35] Similar process-of-elimination reasoning could just as easily land one in any one of the aforementioned professions without any real sense of what is involved in it.

Let's now have a look at Nora's reasons for going to law school in light of these profile observations. "What do you have to know to to go to law school?" she asks. "You don't have to know anything. . . . There were a lot of people like me who went to law school because we graduated from college, maybe we did something for a year or so, and we couldn't figure out what we really wanted to do. Law school was seen as a continuation of our liberal arts education, without having to endure the seven years of agony of graduate school."[36] Remember now, she turned out to be a very successful lawyer. Her choice, haphazard as it was, could well have turned out to be the right one. So, what did she find?

For one thing, the law is no longer a genteel profession. It has become cutthroat and all consuming, especially with the advent of high technology and the alliance of the profession with investment bankers engendering a business mentality.[37] That's one of Nora's misgivings. A more personal complaint is the interference with one's normal life activities. As Kaye puts it:

> If this "interference" must be endured by young lawyers of both sexes, women like Nora seem to resent it more keenly. Nora attributes her survival in the profession to her willingness to "work like a man" and scant the domestic side of her personality. "At [my last firm], you offer up your life as a sacrifice on the altar of the law, and you say, 'I'm yours,' " she says. "Once they have you, if you show any indicia of being a woman, such as getting pregnant, they're really pissed off. [They say], 'You failed us, you reneged on your part of the agreement; you're trying to take back one part of your life, and you belong body and soul to us'."[38]

Nora is facing up to the classic struggle between living to work and working to live. She speaks of "inertia" as one of the reasons she has trouble leaving the law. She doesn't mention her self-identity as a lawyer, but it's clear that is part of the problem. "Harvard Law School was really hard. It takes a lot of courage to say, 'I'm going to do something that uses my law school training only tangentially, if at all.' It's difficult to say, 'I wasted three years of my life.' "[39] Also, "The money is intoxicating. . . . To get to the point where you can say, 'Yeah, I want that' and then just buy it for yourself is quite wonderful in a way."[40] In a way, yes. And in a way, too, Nora, like others of her ilk, is a victim of her own success. Unlike poor, harassed Charles Brockden Brown, however, she has financial and employment opportunities beyond his wildest dreams.

Kaye also tells the more decisive story of James Upchurch, J.D. '75, who gave up a lucrative law practice in Montgomery, Alabama, to try writing for a living, his lifelong dream. He is now publisher and editor of *Montgomery!* magazine. Or Amy Powers, J.D. '87, who quit corporate law to become a lyricist for the musical theater. Through a highly placed Broadway impresario selected by her parents to *discourage* her from such a move, she was instead introduced to Andrew Lloyd Webber with whom she successfully collaborated on a song-and-dance version of *Sunset Boulevard.*[41]

What these and other similar stories of false starts illustrate, among other things, are the personal costs of ignoring the biblical injunction, "Unto thine own self be true." In the words of Juliana Jensen, J.D., '81, an artist and onetime professional dancer who felt herself miscast after five years in the aggressive atmosphere of a San Francisco law firm and gave it all up to become a full-time painter: "In my thirties, I feel much closer to the person I thought I was when I was ten years old. When I was in my twenties, I was trying to be an idea of myself—I don't know whose. Now I'm incredibly happy because I'm leading a more truthful existence in a way."[42] By the same token, I am personally acquainted with frustrated artists, writers, and musicians who went back to law or business schools in order to take up more conventional careers, usually arts related: music publishing or production, museum administration, concert hall management, legal oversight of intellectual and artistic products, and the like. It's less important which way you go after a false start than that the decision be your own and not somebody else's.

CONSOLIDATION

What is the purpose of education? To learn how to think, to do things that may be useful or interesting to us, whether on borrowed interest or for their own sake. Education helps us to order and integrate experience into a palatable life pattern that has mostly to do with what you take most pride in accomplishing: a family well raised, a job well done, a novel published, public service, a sail around the world, a corporate empire sustained, knowledge acquired. Fundamentally, it concerns what you *do*, not something you own or possess. Possessions and acclaim pale before the questions, What do I really want? Why am I doing this? How you answer those questions has everything to do with your character and personality. There is no escaping that. "Life is always worth living," says James, "if one have such responsive sensibilities."

> But we of the highly educated classes (so called) have most of us got far, far away from Nature. We are trained to seek the choice, the rare, the exquisite exclusively, and to overlook the common. We are stuffed with abstract conceptions, and glib verbalities and verbosities; and in the culture of these higher functions the peculiar sources of joy connected with our simpler functions often dry up, and we grow stone-blind and insensible to life's more elementary and general goods and joys.[43]

"Old fogeyism begins at a younger age than we think," adds James in a sardonic moment. "I am almost afraid to say so, but I believe that in the majority of human beings it begins at about twenty-five."[44] And finally,

> So you see that the process of education, taken in a large way, may be described as nothing but the process of acquiring ideas or conceptions, the best educated mind being the mind which has the largest stock of them, ready to meet the largest possible variety of the emergencies of life. The lack of education means only the failure to have acquired them, and the consequent liability to be "floored" and "rattled" in the vicissitudes of experience.[45]

Top that for getting on in life.

SUMMARY

This final chapter began with a series of little histories illustrating how some individuals at different life stages started over. Life is, after all, "a thing of histories," as Dewey reminds us, "each with its own plot, its own inception and movement toward its close, each having its own particular rhythmic movement; each with its own unrepeated quality pervading it throughout."[46] I went on to talk about the reconstruction of the Self on task, a change that repeats and renews itself throughout the life cycle, with attention to what you, as one starting out, can do to assist those starting over, knowing that at some juncture in life, you, too, shall have to start over. I then examined the prospects of "second acts" in a variety of professions, some of which do and some of which don't seem to accommodate follow-up careers in an advisory or consulting capacity.

Some second acts are lateral adjustments of accumulated experience to new fields and enterprises. Others are more abrupt, marking a sharp break with the past. Most involve at least some pain and uncertainty. I made a special plea to those of you starting out to support policies and programs for those starting over, not only for their interests but for yours in the future.

Learning from experience was analyzed in terms of Dewey's distinction between passive recognition and active perception as marking the difference between being trapped by or learning from experience. I then assayed the costs and liabilities of false starts in professional life, often engendered by an urgency to satisfy others' expectations rather than one's own. Finally, I cited James's remarks, as befits a book addressed to graduates in his memory, on our loss of appreciation for the simpler pleasures of life and the value of education to enable us to cope with life's demands. In his generous spirit, I wish you every success and a growth of strategic and moral vision that will make it all worthwhile.

NOTES

1. All the more reason to cultivate your strategic and moral visions from an early stage in your work experience, if not before.

2. *New York Times*, 26 September 1994, p. C2.

3. Ibid.

4. Ibid.

5. F. Scott Fitzgerald, *The Last Tycoon* (1941; New York: Macmillan, 1986), p. 163.

6. Erik H. Erikson, *Childhood and Society* (New York: W. W. Norton, 1963); Erik H. Erikson, *Identity and the Life Cycle* (New York: W. W. Norton, 1980); Erik H. Erikson, *The Life Cycle Completed* (New York: W. W. Norton, 1982).

7. See Chapter 3.

8. William Warner, *Beautiful Swimmers: Watermen, Crabs, and the Chesapeake Bay* (Boston: Little, Brown, 1976).

9. Robert Frost, "The Road Not Taken," in *Great American Poets: Robert Frost*, ed. Geoffrey Moore (New York: Potter, 1986).

10. See Chapter 2.

11. Dewey, *Art as Experience*, p. 37.

12. Ibid., p. 38.

13. Ibid., p. 37.

14. Ibid., pp. 44–45.

15. Ibid., p. 53.

16. Ibid.

17. Ibid.; italics Dewey's.

18. Ibid., p. 54; italics Dewey's.

19. Ibid., pp. 51–52.

20. See Chapter 2, pp. 31–32.

21. For an especially poignant insight into the tragic effects of overweaning parental ambition and coercion, see *The Dead Poet's Society*, starring Robin Williams as a charismatic schoolmaster whose success at teaching poetry has unforeseen consequences.

22. See Chapter 1, pp. 10–11.

23. See Robert A. Ferguson, *Law and Letters in American Culture* (Cambridge: Harvard University Press, 1984), chap. 5, "The Case of Charles Brockden Brown," pp. 129–49. I owe this reference to Jane Garry, my editor at Greenwood Press.

24. Ibid., pp. 129–30.

25. Ibid., pp. 131–32.

26. Ibid., p. 133.

27. Ibid., p. 139.

28. Ibid., p. 147.

29. Howard Gardner, *Extraordinary Minds: Portraits of Exceptional Individuals and an Examination of Our Extraordinariness* (New York: Basic Books, 1997), p. 15.

30. See, for example, David A. Tallman, "Why I Quit Teacher's Education to Go Back to Law School," in *The Long-Term View*, 3, no. 4 (Winter 1997): 62–69.

31. Glenn Kaye, "Free of the Law," *Harvard Magazine* 94, no. 3 (January-February 1992): 60.

32. Ibid., p. 64; italics mine.

33. Ibid., pp. 64–65.

34. Ibid., p. 64.

35. Ibid., p. 66.

36. Ibid.

37. Ibid., p. 63.

38. Ibid., p. 62.

39. Ibid., p. 66.

40. Ibid.

41. Ibid., p. 65. It's worth quoting in full Kaye's interview with Arlene Hirsch, a Chicago psychotherapist, who observes that "few young lawyers seeking new careers can look to their families for understanding—least of all to their parents. 'Some parents derive their self-esteem from what their children are doing,' she says. . . . 'Then there are parents who really do want their children to be happy but who can't understand why their children should be unhappy with this field,' Hirsch continues. 'Often they don't know anything about the law. But the children still feel ungrateful, spoiled, and selfish for wanting to do something different.' "

42. Ibid.

43. James, *Talks*, p. 126.

44. Ibid., p. 79.

45. Ibid., pp. 71–72.

46. Dewey, *Art as Experience*, pp. 35–36.

SELECTED BIBLIOGRAPHY

Aristotle. *Nicomachean Ethics.* J. L. Ackrill, ed. Book 6. London: Faber, 1973.

Collins, Eliza, and Patricia Scott. "Everyone Who Makes It Has a Mentor." *Harvard Business Review* (July-August 1978): 89–101.

Crick, Francis. *What Mad Pursuit: A Personal View of Scientific Discovery.* New York: Basic Books, 1988.

Csikszentmihalyi, Mihalyi. *Flow, The Psychology of Optimal Experience.* New York: Harper & Row, 1990.

Dewey, John. *Art as Experience.* 1934. New York: Putnam, 1958.

Grubb, W. Norton, and Marvin Larzerson. "Rally 'Round the Workplace: Continuities and Fallacies in Career Education." *Harvard Educational Review* 45, no. 4 (1975): 451–74.

Hammer, Michael, and James Champy. *Reengineering the Corporation: A Manifesto for Business Revolution.* New York: Harper Business, 1993.

Hammer, Michael, and Steven A. Stanton. *The Reengineering Revolution: A Handbook.* New York: Harper Business, 1995.

Head, Simon. "The New, Ruthless Economy." *New York Review of Books* 43, no. 4 (29 February 1996): 47–52.

Howard, V. A. *Artistry: The Work of Artists.* Cambridge: Hackett, 1982.

Howard, V. A., ed. *Varieties of Thinking: Essays from Harvard's Philosophy of Education Research Center.* New York: Routledge, 1990.

Howard, V. A. *Learning by All Means: Lessons from the Arts*. New York and Berlin: Peter Lang, 1992.

Howard, V. A., and J. H. Barton. *Thinking Together: Making Meetings Work*. New York: William Morrow, 1992.

Howard, V. A., and Israel Scheffler. *Work, Education, and Leadership*. New York and Berlin: Peter Lang, 1994.

James, William. *Talks to Teachers on Psychology and to Students on Some of Life's Ideals*. 1899. New York: Dover, 1992.

Kaye, Glenn. "Free of the Law." *Harvard Magazine* 94, no. 3 (January-February 1992): 60.

Kennedy, Paul. *Preparing for the Twenty-first Century*. New York: Random House, 1993.

Levinson, Daniel J., with Charlotte N. Darrow, Maria H. Levinson, Edward B. Klein, and Braxton McKee. *The Seasons of a Man's Life*. New York: Ballantine Books, 1978.

Mayer, Nancy. *The Male Mid-Life Crisis: Fresh Starts after Forty*. New York: Doubleday, 1978.

Miller, Nathan. *F.D.R.: An Intimate History*. New York: Doubleday, 1983.

Moore, Kathryn M. "The Role of Mentors in Developing Leaders for Academe." In *Contemporary Issues in Leadership*, ed. William E. Rosenback and Robert L. Taylor (Boulder: Westview Press, 1984).

Polanyi, Michael. *Personal Knowledge*. London: Routledge & Kegan Paul, 1958.

Roche, Gerald. "Much Ado about Mentors." *Harvard Business Review* (January 1979): 14–28.

Russell, Bertrand. *In Praise of Idleness*. 1935. London: Unwin Hyman, 1976.

Scheffler, Israel. *Of Human Potential*. New York: Routledge & Kegan Paul, 1985.

Schiller, Friedrich. *Letters on the Aesthetic Education of Man*. Trans. Reginald Snell. 1796. Reprint, New York: Frederick Ungar, 1965.

Schwartz, Felice N. "Management Women and the New Facts of Life." *Harvard Business Review* (January-February 1989): 65–76.

Shapiro, Eileen C., Florence P. Haseltine, and Mary P. Rose. "Moving Up: Models, Mentors, and the Patron System." *Sloan Management Review* (Spring 1978): 51–58.

Speizer, Jeanne J. "Role Models, Mentors, and Sponsors: The Elusive Concepts." *Signs* (Summer 1981): 691–712.

Wills, Gary. *Certain Trumpets: The Call of Leaders*. New York: Simon & Schuster, 1994.

INDEX

Abilities: dreams and, 70; exceptional, 124–25

Academics: administration and, 76; conformity of, 43

Accountability, vision and, 17

Achievement: of aims, 15–16; practice and, 39, 40; rise to leadership and, 77

Actions, consequences of, 23

Activity: "excess of doing," 119; idleness versus, 35–37

Adaptability: in the corporate environment, 93; to job market, 102–5; to stressful conditions, 107

Added-value services, 99

Advisors. See Mentors

Aesthetic: experience, 33; perception, 120; sense, 33–34; "stamp," 32–33, 118

Aims, 15–16; vision and, 17, 18

Altruism, 19

Ambitions, 75, 78, 79, 80

Amis, Kingsley, 57, 72

Analytical ability, 34

Analytical categories, 20

Analytic vision, 51

Applied research, 49

Apprentice, 59, 60

Apprenticeship, 48, 59–63

Aristotle, 22–23, 24

Art(s), experiential aspects of, 32–33, 34

Artisans, mentor relations, 62

Artists, 5, 75

Aspirations, 71

Assessment, case analysis and, 51, 54

Athletes, mentor relations, 62

Authoritative instruction, 50

Avocational interests, 27–30

Bacon, Sir Francis, 39

Böll, Heinrich, 35–36

Borderless world, 96–99

Borrowed interest, 67–69, 110, 129
Brown, Charles Brockden, 123–24
Burnout, 81–84, 112
Business aims, 16
Buzzwords, 42
Byers, Mark, 127

Capability, motivation and, 70
Capital flow, global, 97
Career(s), 2, 73; changing/starting over, 109–31; false starts, 122–23; live to work/work to live, 40–44, 124–25, 127, 129; shifts in focus, 76–77; transitions, 115–18; values and, 74–80
Case studies, 48, 51–52
Carpe diem, 28
Catching on, 47. See also Apprenticeship; Example; Imitation; Instruction
Champy, James, 94–95
Character: effect on development and career choice, 70–74; employers' expectation of, 104; test of, 74
Chief executive officers (CEOs), 21, 59
Closed exemplars, 53, 58
Collaboration, with mentor, 60
College graduates, employment potential, 99–105
Commitment, 57; organizational mission and, 10
Communication skills, 103–4, 105, 107
Comparison, imitation and, 57
Competence, vision and, 17
Competency, 5, 33
Compromise, 75–76
Computer skills, 104–5

Conceptualization ability, 33
Conduct, norms of, 42
Conformity, 42–43, 44, 56, 125, 126
Connections, idea-application, 73
Context of learning, 3
Co-op education, 3, 37–38
Corporate: aims, 16; image, 42; mission, 10–11
Counseling. See Mentors
Creative thinking, 34, 36–37, 76, 105
Crick, Francis, 42, 74, 77
Critical reflection, 17, 34, 72
Critical skills, strategic vision and, 69
Critical thinking skills, 105
Criticism, mentor's, 59
Curtin, Phyllis, 56, 115

Darwin, Charles, 27, 28, 42
Davis, Bette, 79
Daydreaming, 36, 37
Deliberative knowledge, 22–23
Demonstrations, 52
Design, models and, 54
Dewey, John, 5, 17, 31–32, 33, 36, 73, 118, 119–20
Diagrams, 54
Dialogue: inner, 57–58; professional, 103–4; teacher-student, 49, 50
Discipline(s): catching on to, 47–66; immersion in, 33, 34; social imagery of, 42–43
Discovery method, 51
Dispositions, 70–74
Downsizing, 92, 99
Dreams: abilities and, 70; adapting to reality, 58; ambition and, 80; daydreams, 36, 37; exposure to exemplars

and, 71–72; strategic vision and, 73

Drills. *See* Practice

Drudgery, sustaining interest in face of, 44, 68–69

Education: aims of, 15; college, 102; for work, 44; liberal, 14, 20–22, 109–10; professional, 102; purpose of, 129–30; types of, 30; vocational, 21, 38, 102, 109

Educational leadership, 48

Effort, 28–30

Employee dispensability, 94

Employment, prerequisites, 103

Employment interview, organizational mission and, 10

Ends, 15; connecting means to, 68–69; justifying means, 16

Environmental scanning, 17

Erikson, Erik, 115

Ethical restrictions, 16

Evans, Bill, 39

Example, catching on by, 51–55, 72

Excellence, achievement of, 22–23

Exemplar(s), 53–54, 56, 57–58, 61, 71–72

Expectations, fulfilling other people's, 126–27

Experience(s): control over, 33; creating own, 120; critical analysis of, 34; dispositions arising from, 72; frenetic activity and, 36, 119; guided field, 49; hands-on, 37–38, 49; interpretation based on, 31–33; learning from, 117, 118–22; reconstruction of, 5–6; vision and, 17

Expertise: achieving, 49; practice and, 40; specialists, 34–35; technology of, 52

Extrapolation, professional growth and, 57–58

Facilities, personal: drill and, 38; learning by reference to samples, 53; strategic vision and, 69

Failure: ability to recover from, 125; apprenticeship and, 61–62; burnout and, 82; measured by exemplars, 56; protégé's, 60; reflecting on, 72, 73–74; signposts of, 5

False starts, 122–29

Family life, 78–79

Ferguson, Robert, 123–24

Foreign language skills, 105

Foresight, 14

Frost, Robert, 117–18

Gardner, Howard, 125

Global capital flow, 97

Global competition, 96–99

Goals, 15; burnout and, 82–83; strategic, 19; vision encompassing, 17, 19

Greene, Graham, 81

Growth, opportunities for, 17

Guidance from mentor, 60

Gut feeling, 30–31, 33

Habits, 28, 29, 38, 119

Hammer, Michael, 94–95

Hands-on experience, 37–38, 49

Happiness, 82

Harvard University, Philosophy of Education Research Center, 4

Head, Simon, 89, 92, 94–95, 102

Hecker, Daniel, 99

Hedonic attitude, 68, 70
High school jobs for college graduates, 99–102
Historical vision, 51
Home, working out of, 102–3
Howe, Louis, 60
How-to training, 37, 49, 50

Ideal(s), 53, 61; adapting to reality, 58; extrapolation from, 58; putting skills to work in service of, 71; technical proficiency and, 70
Ideas, technical proficiency and, 70
Identity, work-related, 40–44, 80, 112, 128
Idleness, productivity and, 35–37
Illustrations, case analysis and, 52
Imagination, 14; connections and, 73; relaxation and, 36–37; vision and, 17
Imitation, catching on by, 55–59
Immersion technique: imitation and, 57; mastery and, 33, 34–35
Independent thinking, 31, 34
Influence: leadership versus, 75–78; teaching as a form of, 50
Information: instructing in, 49; technology, 91, 102
Inner dialogue, imitation and, 57–58
Institute on Work and Education (1990), 4
Institutional service, vision and, 17
Instruction: authoritative, 50; catching on by, 48–51; dispositions arising from, 72;

goals requiring, 15; self-, 72; teaching versus, 49–50
Instrumental values, 16
Intellectual leader, 76
Intellectuals, 75
Interest: borrowed, 67–99, 110, 129; keeping alive, 27–30
International companies, 96–99
Interpretation: case analysis and, 51; learning by example and, 54–55
Interpretive abilities, 17, 30–33
Intervention, mentor's, 59
Intuition, 30–31, 33, 39, 40
Ives, Charles, 13

James, William, 4–5, 27–28, 35, 37, 39, 67, 84, 130
Job market, adaptability to, 102–5
Job training programs, 102
Judgment: apex of powers and, 73; case analysis and, 51; failure and, 73–74; interpretive, 30–33; open exemplars and, 53–54, 57; mentor's, 61; training and, 38; vision and, 17

Kant, Immanuel, 30
Kaye, Glenn, 125–26, 128–29
Kennedy, Paul, 96, 98, 100
Kenney, Douglas C., 68, 70
Know-how, 49, 50
Knowledge: applying general, 31; Aristotle's taxonomy of, 22–23; changes in, 5; deliberative, 22–23; intuition and, 39, 40; mentor's, 61; personal interests and, 27–30; practical, 23; productive, 22, 30, 74; self-transformation in ac-

quiring, 73; theoretical, 22, 23

Lawyers, career changes of, 125–29
Lay-offs, 111
Leadership, influence versus, 75–78
Learning: by apprenticeship, 48, 59–63; on borrowed interest, 67–69, 110, 129; breaks in rhythm of, 47; content of, 20; context of, 3; direction of, 20; by doing, 37–38, 49; by example, 51–55, 72; from experience, 117, 118–22; by imitation, 55–59; inducement, 29; by instruction, 48–51; instrumental, 13, 14, 15, 16; intrinsic motivation and, 13; mental hygiene of, 4–5; personal interests and, 27–30; practice and, 37–40; with purpose, 14–20, 23, 41; role of sensibilities in, 30–37; Schiller's categories, 30; utilitarian, 67; value attached to, 13; values shaping and controlling, 5; willingness and, 34; at work, 3; for work, 1
Legal restrictions, 16
Letters on the Aesthetic Education of Man (Schiller), 30
Liberal arts graduates, advantages of, 20–22, 109–10
Liberal education, product of, 14
Life changes, ambition and, 80
Life's work. *See* Vocation
Lincoln, Abraham, 75
Listening skills, 104
"Little daily tax," 27–46
Living standard, 89–90
Lombardi, Vince, 59

MacArthur, Douglas, 17–18, 30
Management process schemes, 19–20
Mandel Institute for Advanced Studies in Education, 48–49, 62
Manufacturing industry, 91, 102
Mastery, practice and, 37–40
Material rewards, 78
Mathematical aptitude, music and, 22
Mayer, Nancy, 82, 83
Means: connecting to ends, 67–69; ends justifying, 16
Means-ends continuum, 17
Mental hygiene of learning, 4–5
Mentors, 58, 116, 122; mentor-protégé relation, 59–64
Military connotations, organizational missions and, 9–10
Missions, 9–25
Model, mentor as, 61
Models, 54
Morality, learning for, 30
Moral: perspective, 74; responsibility, 44; standards, 69, 74; virtue, 74; vision, 18–19, 22, 41, 44, 76, 83–84
Motivation, 13, 75; capability and, 70
Multinational companies, 96–99
Music, mathematical aptitude and, 22

National Center for Research on Vocational Education, 4
New England Conservatory (NEC), 21–22, 23
Norm(s), professional, 42
Normative conditions, aims and, 15–16

Objectives, strategic, 15

Observation, case analysis and, 51

Open exemplars, 53–54, 57–58

Organizational mission, 9–25

Outsourcing, 91

Passmore, John, 56

People skills, 76, 103–4, 107

Perception, 119–20

Performance standards, 69, 71, 74

Personal choices, range of, 3

Personal example, 55

Personal relationships, careers and, 78–79

Personality: developmental course and, 27–30, 70–74; expression of, 34; innovators, 125; reasons for working and, 130; telephone, 103

Perspective, 44; moral, 74

Philosophic vision, 51

Picasso, Pablo, 75

Pleasurable activities, 27–30, 79

Politicians, as mentors, 61–62

Positive reinforcement, 72

Practice: catching on by, 48; goals requiring, 15; guided, 51; imitation and, 58; interpretive abilities increasing with, 17; training versus, 38–40; value of, 37–40

Practices, extrapolation from, 57–58

Preventive conditions, goal realization and, 15

Principles, applying general, 31

Problem solving, 15, 105; ability in, 20; case study and, 51; group, 103

Procedures: aims and, 15, 16; learning by imitation, 55, 58; norms of, 42

Production, reengineering, 91

Productivity, 102; idleness and, 35–37; software packages increasing, 95; wages and, 90–91

Profession, catching on to, 47–66

Professional: conduct, 107; jargon, 42; judgment, 50; norms, 42; opportunities versus personal interests, 28; practices, social imagery of, 42–43; range of, 3

Promotions, 77–78

Public presentation, ability to make, 104

Reality, adapting dreams and ideals to, 58

Reality checks, 37

Real world, toughing out, 89–108

Recognition, bare, 119

Reengineering, 91–96, 99

Reengineering czar, 92–96

Reflection, 36; critical, 34, 72; daydreaming and, 37; failure and, 73–74; innovators using, 125

Reflective effort, 30

Reich, Robert, 90

Relaxation, 35, 36–37, 81

Religious connotations, organizational missions and, 9–10

Research scientists, 76

Restructuring, 94

Retirement, and new careers, 113–15

Retraining, 102

Rewards, 77; conformity and, 127; material, 78

Richard, Larry, 127

Rohatyn, Felix, 90, 91, 93

Roosevelt, Franklin D., 58, 60, 61, 62, 75

Routines: drill and, 38; learning by imitation, 55, 58; mastery of, 37–40; streamlining, 91–96
Russell, Bertrand, 76

Samples, 52–53
Samuelson, Robert, 100
Schiller, Friedrich, 30–31
Scholars, 11, 75–76
School/work divide, transformations across, 20–23
Schwartz, Felice N., 78–79
Scientific careers, 11
Self: constricted, 41–42; investment in, 13–14; moral vision and, 19; reconstruction of, 3, 112; transformation of, 5, 20–23, 40–44
Self-deception, 124
Self-development, 11–14, 41, 70–74
Self-esteem, 13, 41, 81
Self-identity, work and, 40–44, 78–80, 112, 128
Self-instruction, 72
Self-motivation, 13
Sensibilities: role in learning, 30–37, 130; shaped by teaching, 50
Service industries, 92, 102–3
Shanker, Albert, 18–19
Shaw, Bernard, 81
Simulations, 52
Skill(s): changes in, 5; computer, 104–5; employer's wish list of, 20, 103; foreign language, 105; high school, 99–100; instructing in, 49; learning by imitation, 55, 58; liberal arts graduates, 20; low-wage jobs, 100–101; objectives for, 15; obsolete, 38, 92, 95; people, 76, 103–4; put-

ting to work in service of ideals, 71; technical, 50–51, 69–70, 90–91
Skilled workers, decline in need for, 92
Smith, Al, 61–62
Social imagery, professional, 42–43
Socrates, 50, 71, 76
Software packages, replacing jobs, 92, 93, 95
Solow, Robert, 90
Solti, Sir Georg, 17, 34, 53
Specialists, 20–21, 34–35, 92, 93
Standards: exemplars setting, 53, 61; moral, 69, 74; performance, 69, 71, 74; strategic vision and, 69
Starting over, 109–33
Stern, Isaac, 77
Stevens, Wallace, 13
Strategic ends or objectives, aims as, 15
Strategic goals, 19
Strategic vision, 18, 22, 41, 44, 69, 73
Stress, 2, 75, 107
Style, substance versus, 43
Subject, feel for, 30
Substance, style versus, 43
Success: apprenticeship and, 61–62; burnout and, 81–83; factors, 15; measuring by exemplars, 56; personality and, 70–74; protégé's, 60; signposts of, 5; vision and, 17
Supranationals, 96
Symbolic representation, 54

Tactical goals, 15
Talent, hidden, 72
Talks to Teachers on Psychology and to Students on Some of

Life's Ideals (James), 4–5, 27–28

Task(s): coaching in, 59; drudgery associated with, 68–69; feel for, 30; immersion in, 5, 33, 34–35; identifying with, 57–58; instructing in, 50; maintaining interest in difficult, 67–87; owning, 71; practicing, 37–40

Taste, 30, 31, 50

Teaching, instruction versus, 49–50

Technical: fields, 21; proficiency, 50–51, 69–70, 73, 90–91

Technocrats, 92–96

Technological aristocracy, 92–96

Technology: of expertise, 52; information, 91, 102

Telephone personality, 103

Terminations, 111

Theories, revision of, 29

Thought: creative, 34, 36–37, 76, 105; feeling and, 30; idle, 35–37; independent, 31, 34; reflective, 36

Training: continuity of, 40; drill versus, 38–40; educating for work versus, 44; how-to, 37, 49, 50; innovations, 58; instruction and, 50; mid-life, 116

Transformations: becoming what you do, 40–44; professional norms and, 42–43; of self, 5, 20–23

Transitions, 1, 115–18

Understanding: beginning of, 47; learning for, 30

Unemployment, 90, 95, 99, 102, 111

Unions, 90, 91

Utilitarian learning, 67

Values, 3; aims and, 16; conflicting, 79; instrumental, 16; moral vision and, 18, 19; shaping and controlling learning, 5; work's changing, 74–80

Vision, 14, 17–19; analytic, 51; historical, 51; mentor's, 58, 61; moral, 18–19, 22, 41, 44, 76, 83–84; philosophic, 51; as predictive faculty, 17; productive knowledge and, 30; strategic, 18, 22, 41, 44, 69, 73; shaped by teaching, 50

Vocation, 10–11, 43; dreams and, 71–72; living for, 79–80; moral vision and, 18

Vocational education, 21, 38, 102, 109

Vogt, Leona, 126

Wages, 90–91, 99–102

Watson, James, 74

Wills, Garry, 75, 76

Wilson, Woodrow, 58–59

Wittgenstein, Ludwig, 30, 33, 43, 55

Women, careers and, 78–79

Work: addictive, 79; burnout and, 81–84, 112; changing values of, 74–80; educating for, 44; high school jobs for college graduates, 99–102; identification with, 40–44; identity derived from, 80, 112, 128; learning at, 3; living to, 78–80, 128; reshaping self for, 3

Work-study programs, 37–38

World, borderless, 96–99

About the Author

V. A. HOWARD has been Co-Director of the Philosophy of Education Research Center at Harvard University since 1983. He has published widely on the arts and education, music aesthetics, and learning. His previous books include, *Artistry: the Work of Artists* (1982); *Thinking on Paper* (with J. H. Barton, 1992); *Learning by all Means: Lessons From the Arts* (1992); and *Work, Education, and Leadership* (with Israel Scheffler, 1994).